THE GOSPEL
ACCORDING TO

ELVIS

THE GOSPEL
ACCORDING TO

ELVIS

KEVIN & TANJA CROUCH

**BOBCAT
BOOKS**

LONDON / NEW YORK / PARIS / SYDNEY / COPENHAGEN / BERLIN / MADRID / TOKYO

Order No: BOB 11539R
ISBN 13: 978.1.86074.655.0
ISBN 10: 1.86074.655.1

Exclusive Distributors
Music Sales Limited,
14–15 Berners Street,
London W1T 3LJ

Music Sales Corporation,
257 Park Avenue South,
New York, NY 10010, USA.

Macmillan Distribution Services,
53 Park West Drive,
Derrimut, Vic 3030,
Australia.

Every effort has been made to trace the copyright holders of the photographs
in this book but one or two were unreachable. We would be grateful if the
photographers concerned would contact us.

Printed and bound by Gutenberg Press Ltd, Malta

A catalogue record for this book is available from the British Library.

Visit Omnibus Press on the web at www.omnibuspress.com

Contents

Introduction

Dick Clark aptly stated, "It's rare when an artist's talent can touch an entire generation of people. It's even rarer when that same influence affects several generations. Elvis made an imprint on the world of pop music unequalled by any other single performer."

Elvis. You can say that one name almost anywhere in the world, and the inhabitants there will instantly know exactly whom you mean. Rather, they know his legend. It is the classic tale of the American Dream: the boy from the wrong side of the tracks who attained success and fame beyond his wildest imaginings.

Born January 8, 1935 in a two-room shotgun shack in Tupelo, Mississippi, Elvis Aron Presley survived his stillborn twin brother to grow up an only child. Sweet, shy and unusually close to his mother, Elvis passed his unremarkable school years in Memphis, Tennessee, where his life revolved around family and church. Like millions of other youths his age, there was nothing special about Elvis to indicate any destiny beyond the obscurity of his present circumstances; nothing to hint that he was soon to change the course of music history and become one of the most influential figures of twentieth century popular culture.

His career began in a tiny storefront recording studio in 1954. Two years later, Elvis was an international sensation. Then came the gold, platinum and multi-platinum awards for 149 different albums and singles, totalling more than one billion record sales worldwide. There were 14 Grammy Award nominations, three wins, and the Lifetime Achievement Award at age 36. There were starring roles in 33 films, groundbreaking television appearances and specials, and record-breaking concert tours and Las Vegas engagements. The career ended on August 16, 1977, but Elvis himself had long before passed into the realm of legend.

Those who know the legend remember Elvis for his talent, good looks, sensuality, and charisma. Those who knew the man speak of his humility, generosity, and spirituality. Both images are true. Elvis himself recognised the incongruity of his dual nature, but always believed that his life had a deeper purpose and meaning. He said as much in a comment made to a reporter in the earliest days of his success: "I ain't no saint, but I've tried never to do anything that would hurt my family or offend God . . . I figure all any kid needs is hope and the feeling that he or she belongs. If I could do or say anything that would give some kid that feeling, I would believe I had contributed something to the world."

The Gospel According to Elvis celebrates the life of legendary pop icon Elvis Presley with inspirational quotes and anecdotes. Organised into six thematic chapters – Life, Love, Success, Family, Work and Friends – each section includes biographical stories interspersed with quotes from Elvis and topical facts about his life. Additionally, a biography of his life and career, a comprehensive "songography" that lists every recording Elvis made, and a "filmography" that provides an overview of his acting roles round out the book.

In 1956, when his entire career still lay before him, Elvis said, "I always felt that someday, somehow, something would happen to change everything for me, and I'd daydream about how it would be." *The Gospel According to Elvis* traces the story of how the daydream became a reality, and how one young boy with a talent he did not understand managed to skyrocket to unimaginable fame. This book is for everyone who has ever dreamed a dream that was bigger than their own limitations.

The Gospel

FAMILY

Joy and Sadness

- Elvis Aron Presley was born in Tupelo, Mississippi on 8 January 1935. It was a joyous event for his parents, Vernon and Gladys, but it was also a day of overwhelming sadness: Elvis' twin, Jesse Garon, was stillborn just minutes earlier. Some speculate the tragedy was due to the fact the family was too poor to afford medical care. "My little brother died," recalled Elvis, "and my mama almost died because we couldn't afford to go to the hospital."

The Bond Between Mother and Son

- Elvis and his mother, Gladys, had a powerful bond that no one could come between. Her belief in Elvis gave him the confidence to pursue his dream to make music professionally. "Everyone loves their mother, but I was an only child, and mother was always right there with me. All my life . . ." Her death was painful and left a void. "It wasn't like losing a mother, it was like losing a friend, a companion, someone to talk to. I could wake her up any hour of the night if I was worried or troubled by something. She'd get up and try to help me. I used to get very angry at her when I was growing up. It's only natural when a young person wants to go somewhere or do something and your mother won't let you – to think, 'why, what's wrong with you?' But later on in the years, you know, you find out that she was right. That she was only doing it to protect you and keep you from getting in any trouble and from getting hurt. And I'm very happy that she was kinda strict on me, very happy that it worked out the way it did."

Right and Wrong

- "Mama never could do enough for me. She took me to all those church meetings every Sunday to make sure I didn't ever go wrong." Years after Gladys's death, Elvis reflected, "I still think of her every single, solitary day. If I never do anything that's really wrong or bad, it'll be because of Mama. She wouldn't never let me do anything wrong."

Early Air Guitar

- "I never took any singing lessons and the only practicing I ever did was on a broom stick before my dad gave me my first guitar."

Grace

- Elvis was able to sustain a sense of personal grace that prevented him from getting caught up in some of the pitfalls of wealth and fame. "I've always considered other people's feelings; I've always treated people just like I would like to be treated." Elvis attributed his gracious nature to his parents: "It's the way I was brought up . . . My mother and father – the whole family – were always considerate of other people's feelings. I am proud of the way I was brought up to believe and to treat people. I have respect for people."

Return on Investment

- "I was strumming the guitar before I came to Memphis. My father bought one for $12 – it was the best investment he ever made."

6

The Check Is in the Mail

- On November 26, 1954, Elvis sent a Western Union money order and telegram to his parents that read: "Hi Babies, Here's the money to pay the bills. Don't tell no one how much I sent. I will send more next week. There is a card in the mail. Love Elvis." Always generous, as fame and fortune increased, Elvis repaid his parents' love and devotion with a life of luxury.

The Family Business

- Several of Elvis' family members found gainful employment working for him. His father, Vernon, who had struggled to find and keep a job that would support his family during Depression times became business manager to his multi-millionaire son. "My father takes care of all my personal needs," Elvis explained to a reporter, ". . . all the personal business, banking, any business transactions – he handles it all." Cousin Patsy was hired to assist Vernon. "Billy, who is my little cousin . . . he had to quit school early to get a job. He had a hard time finding a job because of his size, so I gave him a job . . . He does little odd jobs." Maternal Grandmother Minnie Mae – or "Dodger", as Elvis called her – lived at Graceland, as did Minnie's widowed daughter Delta. Over the years, numerous other family members – as well as friends who became kin – were given employment, lived at Graceland, or benefited in other ways by Elvis' generosity.

Miss Manners

- "My mother always taught me to behave, to have good manners; to help people, not harm them; to work hard and never give up, and to make it on my own."

That's Life

- Gladys died on 14 August, 1958, while Elvis was serving in the US Army. She never saw many of her son's achievements, but she did get to see his meteoric success before he was drafted. He lavished gifts upon her – things she never dreamed of owning – a brand new pink Cadillac, clothes, and Graceland. "Funny, she never really wanted anything, you know, anything fancy," Elvis recalled. "She just stayed the same all the way through the whole thing. I wish, you know – there's a lot of things [that have] happened since she passed away, that I wish she could have been around to see; that would have made her very happy and very proud. But, that's life . . ."

The Simple Things in Life

- To the world he was ELVIS!, but at heart he was just a typical guy, with a typical guy's yearning to love and be loved. "I'd like to have a family. It's a normal thing to do. Who wants to go home and be alone?"

Baby Let's Play House

- "I would like to get married. I would like to have a family," Elvis told Lloyd Shearer in 1962. Five years later, he finally married Priscilla Beaulieu on May 1, 1967. Weeks after their marriage, Elvis and Priscilla received news she was pregnant. Though it was a shock to both of them, Elvis told the press, "This is the greatest thing that has ever happened to me. We really hadn't planned to have a baby this soon. [When] Priscilla told me the good news . . . [at first] I was so shocked I didn't think I could move for a while. Then it began to dawn on me this is what marriage is all about." Lisa Marie Presley was born February 1, 1968.

Fatherly Advice

- Fatherhood was still six years in the future when interviewer Lloyd Shearer asked Elvis what advice he would tell his son if he had one. "I think my biggest thing would be consideration for other people – the thing I was taught – consideration for other people's feelings. In doing that, you can keep yourself from becoming hard, therefore making you a better human being." Elvis never had a son. His daughter, Lisa Maria, was his only child. She wrapped her father around her finger and became the terror of Graceland. Whenever she saw a married member of her father's entourage with a girl sitting on his lap, she would threaten to fire him or tell his wife if he didn't do as she asked.

Mama

- Elvis and his mother Gladys were unusually close. Possibly a result of the loss she felt over the stillborn birth of Elvis' twin, Jesse Garon, Gladys was extremely protective of Elvis, nearly smothering him. "My mama never let me out of her sight," Elvis stated. "I couldn't go down to the creek with the other kids. Sometimes when I was little, I used to run off. Mama would whip me, and I though she didn't love me."

Staying Connected

- Gladys Presley deeply missed her son when he was off touring the country. A good son, Elvis telephoned her daily to share his experiences and tell her he loved her. ". . . she is always worried about me," he said. ". . . she is not in real good health . . . and if she worries too much, it might not be good for her, so I make it a habit of calling home every day or so."

Happy Ending

- "My daddy never made much money, but I don't remember ever wanting something real bad that he wouldn't try to get it for me." The Presleys were poor. Very poor. When Elvis was born, his parents were living in a two-room shack. Vernon drifted from job to job. Once when the family was nearly starving to death, he tried to shoplift some groceries. He was caught and arrested. Gladys was forced to beg food from neighbours. Another time, Vernon and two friends forged a $4 check to pay for a hog. Caught and convicted, Vernon served nine months in prison. While he was away, his family lost their home and took refuge with Vernon's parents. "I know what poverty is," Elvis said, "I lived it for a long time." Through all the adversity, the family remained close. "All my life I've always had a nice time," he said of his childhood. "We didn't have any money or nothing, but always managed. We never had any luxuries, but . . . we were never hungry. That's something to be thankful for, even if you don't have all the luxuries, because there are so many people who don't." Another time Elvis summed up his childhood, saying, "We were always happy as long as we were together."

The Good Life

- "I've got daddy some suits that he never had before . . . Mother goes to town now and she buys anything she wants, which makes me feel real good."

Better than a Postcard

- "I buy a lot of little gadgets for the home when I'm out travelling around and send them home. Mother always puts them up. It makes me feel a little more like I'm there with them."

Home Sweet Home

- "Maybe some day I'm going to have a home and a family of my own, and I'm not going to budge from it. I was an only child, but maybe my kids won't be. I suppose this kind of talk raises another question: Am I in love? No. I thought I [was] in love, but I guess I wasn't. It just passed over. I guess I haven't met the girl yet – but I will. And I hope it won't be too long because I get lonesome sometimes. I get lonesome right in the middle of a crowd 'cause I've got a feeling that with her, whoever she may be, I won't be lonesome no matter where I am."

Gladys is Gone

- "I knew what it was before I answered," said Elvis of his father's call to tell him that Gladys had passed away. Both men were inconsolable. The next day, he leaned over her grave and cried out, "Goodbye, darling, goodbye. I love you so much. You know how much I lived my whole life just for you." He later commented, "Everything I have is gone . . ." His epitaph for her gravestone seemed to sum up his feelings: "Thy will, not mine, be done."

Mama Liked the Roses

- "The bottom dropped out of my life the day my mother died. I thought that I had nothing left. In a way I was right." Throughout 1960 and 1961, whenever Elvis was in Memphis, he visited his mother's grave twice a week. He arranged to have red roses placed at her grave each week and if he were in town, he delivered them himself.

Mother's Last Request

- "One of the last things mom said was that daddy and I should always be together, so whenever they send me, daddy will go too." Vernon served as personal/business

manager for Elvis and remained an important part of his
life until his son's untimely death on 16 August 1977.

We All Need Somebody to Lean On

- Currie Grant was the entertainment director at the Eagle
  Club, a community centre for air force families stationed
  in Weisbanden, Germany. He was also the man who
  introduced Priscilla Beaulieu to Elvis Presley. Captain
  Beaulieu allowed his 14-year-old daughter to attend a
  gathering at Elvis' home in Germany, chaperoned by
  Currie Grant and his wife, but only after he had checked
  out Grant. He then insisted Priscilla be home by
  11 o'clock – it was after all, a school night. There was an
  immediate connection between Elvis and Priscilla. Friends
  who were there say he was instantly smitten. The girl of
  his dreams had walked into his life. "I want to be alone
  with you, Priscilla," he told her. "I swear, I'll never do
  anything to harm you." Elvis was able to confide in
  Priscilla and she seemed to fill the void of loneliness he felt.
  "I happen to be very fond of her," Elvis told her father. "I
  guess you might say I need someone to talk to. You don't
  have to worry about her. I'll take good care of her."

Mother and Child

- "The most beautiful thing in the world to me is a baby
  lookin' as pretty as her mama."

Daddy's Girl

- From the moment she arrived, Elvis adored his daughter
  Lisa Marie. "Oh, man, she's just great! I'm still a little
  shaky. She's a doll, she's great – I felt all along she'd be a
  girl." As she grew older, the connection between father
  and daughter grew even stronger. After Elvis and Priscilla
  divorced, he was determined to maintain his connection

with his daughter. She shuttled between Graceland and her mother's home in Southern California. Lisa Marie was at Graceland the night her father died.

I Love You Because . . .

- Speaking of his daughter, Elvis said, "I would like her to remember, and be remembered for, the lady she will become, not for what she'll acquire." He did not always heed his own advice. Lisa Maria had her father wrapped around her finger. If a toy broke, it was magically replaced within 24 hours. When she wanted a puppy, everyone got up immediately and went to buy her one. By the time she was five, she had fur coats and jewellery to rival the most glamorous Hollywood stars.

Fatherhood

- "You realise you're not a kid anymore," Elvis said of being a father. "You have to grow up fast."

Parenting Tips

- Speaking of children, Elvis counselled: "They come first . . . the most precious thing in life. A parent should do anything it takes to give a child a sense of family."

Life On – and Off – the Road

- "It's pretty hard work, travelling the way I've been doing. I've been to a lot of places, but I haven't seen any of them, really. Lots of times all I get to see of the city is a hotel room, my dressing room, and the stage. I don't mind the hard work – I don't guess anybody would mind it after all the good things that's happening to me – the only part I don't like is staying away from home so much. The happiest times I've had have been with my family. In fact, I can't wait to get home every once in a while to be with my mother and daddy. We all have fun together. We sit around and watch television, go to movies, and go for drives on Sunday afternoons . . ."

Have I Told You Lately That I Love You

- Elvis offered this counsel for a happy home and marriage: "Always take that extra few minutes to leave your home in order. Take the time with your wife. Don't take her for granted." Good advice.

One Wish

- "If I could have one wish granted, it would be to talk again with my mother. There are times I dream about her. She's always happy and smiling. Sometimes we embrace, and it's so real I wake up in a cold sweat."

Take Me Home

- The first two years of Elvis' career were filled with recording, touring, press and radio interviews, television performances, and acting. When asked what he did in his spare time, he answered, "I haven't got any – really. When I do get some time off . . . I always go home and see my folks . . ."

Hometown Homecoming

- It was important to Elvis that his family and friends approved of him, particularly those back home in Memphis. It was reported that he was afraid of what the people in his home town might think of his first recording. "I was," he said, "when my first record came out, I was a little leery of it. I thought people would laugh." Instead, they rushed into stores to buy it. Several hits later, he returned to Memphis to play at Ellis Auditorium, on May 15, 1956. Two weeks prior, he told *Press-Scimitar* reporter Bob Johnson: "I want the folks back home to think right of me. Just because I managed to do a little something, I don't want anyone back home to think I got the big head." Six weeks later he gave a concert in Memphis to benefit local charities.

There's No Place Like Home

- During his army stint in Germany, Elvis reminisced on the telephone with Memphis DJ Keith Sherriff and taped the following message for friends and fans back home: "I'd like to say they'll never know how wonderful good old Memphis is until they get away from it for quite a while. And I'm just counting the days and the hours until I can return and sort of pick up where I left off . . . that's all [that's] on my mind, that's all I think about, that's all my heart is set on – and I'll make it."

Who's In Charge?

- "Colonel Parker is more or less like a daddy when I'm away from my folks," Elvis explained to *New York Herald-Tribune* columnist Joe Hyams in May 1957. "He doesn't meddle in my affairs. Ain't nobody can tell me 'you do this or that.' Colonel Parker knows the business and I don't. He never butts into record sessions; I don't butt into business. Nobody can tell you how to run your life." The truth was, Parker often voiced his disapproval of choices Elvis made, particularly when it came to women and how he spent his money, and locked him into movie and publishing contracts that diminished his creative opportunities.

Yes, Sir

- "Sure, Colonel. Whatever you say is okay with me."

Step Mom

- "She seems a pretty nice, understanding type person,"

Elvis said of stepmother Dee Stanley Presley a day or two after she married his father. He went on to tell a reporter for the *Memphis Press-Scimitar*. "She treats me with respect, just as she does daddy. She realises she could never be my mother. I only had one mother and that's it. There'll never be another. As long as she understands that, we won't have any trouble." And of his father, "If he can find happiness in some way, I'm all for him . . . He is my father, and he's all I got left in the world. I'll never go against him or stand in his way. He stood by me all these years and sacrificed things he wanted so that I could have clothes and lunch money to go to school. I'll stand by him now – right or wrong." That is what Elvis told the press. But he was not happy that the couple had carried on an affair while Stanley was still married. He did not attend the wedding. Instead, Elvis went boating. Prior to the marriage, the deed to Graceland, which was in the name of Gladys and Vernon, was put into Elvis' name.

Home Is Where the Heart Is

- Elvis said he would never sell Graceland. Although he owned other houses, Graceland was his home: "the residence of the heart." Most of his family memories, particularly those of his mother, were at Graceland. "It's like seeing and being with her again," he told columnist May Mann. "It is far more than a place of physical needs . . . To me my home is all wound up with all the acts of kindness and gentleness that my mother and my grandmother and my daddy lovingly provided . . . All of this love still remains within its walls. It's an enduring way of life for me." Graceland remains in the possession of the Presley family, including Priscilla and Lisa Maria.

Goin' Back to Graceland

- "Hollywood: a lovely city . . . but home for me will always spell Memphis and Graceland."

FRIENDSHIP

Here Comes Santa Claus

- "We weren't the only family who was thankful to have a Christmas basket of groceries," Elvis recalled of his youth – quite the opposite of Christmas at Graceland. Like everything at Graceland, Christmas was over-the-top. One Christmas Elvis bought Priscilla a black quarter horse named Domino. Then he went in search of a palomino for himself. That led him to buy horses for his family, friends, his entourage and their wives and families – and almost anyone else who came to Graceland. And if you're going to have horses, you need bridles, custom saddles and blankets, and a barn to stable them in. "There is a lot of difference in Christmases today and when we were growing up in East Tupelo. [But] honestly, I can't say these are any better. We are just in a better position to spend. But that's not the important thing. It's the friend-ships and the devotion that really count. Everything is so dreamy when you are young. After you grow up it kind of becomes – just real."

The Memphis Mafia

- The entourage Elvis travelled with became known as "The Memphis Mafia". They were friends and family that handled personal and business chores for him. "I prefer to think of them as members of a little country club I run," he said. "Most of them are my friends from back home . . .

One is my accountant; another's my travel consultant. I need a valet, a security officer, and a wardrobe man with me nearly all the time." On another occasion he explained, "This is my corporation which travels with me all the time. More than that, all these members of my corporation are my friends."

Surround Yourself
- Referring to his friends, his gang known as the "Memphis Mafia," Elvis tells interviewer Lloyd Shearer, "[it's] important to surround yourself with people who can give you a little happiness."

Friends for Life
- "You make friends in the army that you'll remember the rest of your life."

Does Money Buy Friends?
- Asked about the happiest thing about fame and fortune, Elvis said, "The happiest thing . . . I would say money, in a way, of course. That, as you said, is the biggest part, but actually the thing I like is knowing that you have so many friends . . . so many friends . . . you can help. In other words . . . I have a lot of real close fans that I have made since I've been in the business."

Let's Be Friends
- "I wonder how many of my friends that are here now would be here if it were five years ago. Not very many, because they are all looking for something from me."

Wisdom Versus Intellect
- They became known as the "Memphis Mafia". They were the five (although the number grew to as many as eight or nine, at times) men closest to Elvis. They were employed

to entertain, provide companionship, and service his every whim 24-hours a day. Some were relatives, others were friends, but they all became his family. He was often questioned about them – what they did for him and why he had them around. Interviewer Lloyd Shearer questioned Elvis about them and about surrounding himself with those who could provide intellectual growth. "They're pretty smart boys," Elvis answered. "They've learned a lot just being around this industry, being around travelling. Now you can surround yourself with intellectuals or people [who are] your so-called equal[s], and there can be dissension, there can be jealousy, and that's bad. The only thing you can learn there is to become bitter, and envy . . . I have my own way of learning. I learn from the people I work with. I learn from everyday life itself [and] being connected with a lot of different people. But [in] my private and personal life . . . I'm not trying to impress anybody by having a group of intellectuals around – not that I'm knocking [intellectuals], but you can be fooled by having a group of people that you think you're learning from, and you're not learning a damn thing . . . I had a girl say to me one night, 'Don't make the mistake, Elvis, of surrounding yourself with people you can't learn something from,' and the girl never caught it, but I got up and walked away from her. I never said a word, but in so many words I was saying, 'I can't learn anything from you.'"

Friendly Conversation
- "Friends are people you can talk to . . . without words, when you have to."

A Note of Thanks
- In a 1956 recorded message to his fans, Elvis expressed his gratitude for their support: "I want to thank all of my loyal

fans that watch my performances and that way became friends of mine. I sure appreciate your listening to my RCA Victor Records. I'd like to thank all of the disc jockeys for playing them. Bye, bye."

She's a Friend

- "There was a little girl that I was seeing quite often over there . . . and she was at the airport when I left, and there were some pictures made of her. But it was no big romance." That is the story Elvis told the press when he returned to the States after his release from the army. But the two continued to speak on the telephone and exchange letters for a few months before he flew her from Germany for a Christmas visit with him at Graceland. Three months later, he convinced her parents to allow her to live at Graceland, chaperoned by his father and step-mother, while she finished her senior year of high school. "[Her parents] sent her ahead because she wanted to grad-uate on time," Elvis told the press, "she's attending Immaculate Conception High School . . . she's a friend."

Steadfast, Loyal and True

- "Loyalty is the most important thing you can give some-one. Truth, trust, friendship, and very often love all depend on it."

Sincerely

- Throughout his career, Elvis remained as loyal to his fans as they were to him. He was always kind and respectful of them. "I consider other people's feelings," he told Lloyd Shearer in a 1962 interview. "I don't assume the attitude of 'Get these people out of here,' like I have heard of being done . . . Those people are sincere in their feelings . . . they want autographs and pictures . . . I don't just sign the autographs and the pictures, and so forth, to have my popularity, or to make them like me. I do it because I know that they are sincere. They see you and they want an autograph to take home; they got an autograph book or they got their own camera . . . if you don't do it, well, you make them mad at you. They don't understand – you hurt their feelings; you make a lot of enemies that way. And for no reason, because it's as simple as this: . . . once you get involved in this racket – business – your life is public."

Be Cool

- Whether you were friend, family, fan or employee, loyalty was crucial in having a relationship with Elvis. Hired on a whim, shortly after putting Charlie Hodge on the payroll, Elvis told him: "Charlie, as long as you're cool . . . we can be friends."

You're Out

- "It isn't difficult to discover who your real friends are if they're around long enough. If I find out someone sticks with me just to see what he can get out of it, I ease him out of the circle."

Sharing Interests

- When Elvis became interested in a hobby or activity, he included everyone in the fun. After giving Priscilla a horse one Christmas, he bought himself one and proceeded to buy everyone around him a horse. In about two week's time, he spent over $100,000 on his new interest. "I'm having fun, daddy, for the first time in ages," he told his father, when Vernon tried to put a cap on the spending. "I've got a hobby, something I look forward to getting up in the morning for." He was having fun – and so was everyone around him.

Show a Little Kindness

- "I've tried to be the same all through this thing. Naturally, you learn a lot about people and you're involved in a lot of different situations. But, I've tried to be the same. I mean, the way I was brought up, you know, I've always considered other people's feelings. In other words, I didn't kick anybody on the way and I've always treated people just like I would like to be treated."

A Little Help from Some Friends

- While rehearsing a dance number for *Jailhouse Rock,* a cap from one of Elvis' recently fixed teeth came loose and was inhaled, lodging in his lung. He was taken to Cedars of Lebanon Hospital where the cap was removed. Two days later he wrote to the hospital staff, expressing his gratitude for their care: "Dear Friends, I want you to know how very much I appreciate your very wonderful treatment while I was there. When I went in I was 'All Shook Up', but I left 'Loving You'. Thanks a million. My best to all, Sincerely, Elvis Presley."

Liberace!

- While playing Las Vegas, Elvis met the wild and wonderful Liberace. The two became good friends and Liberace even advised Elvis on his stage clothes and performance. "Man, if I could ever get people to talk about me the way they talk about Liberace," Elvis said of his friend, "I would really have it made."

Spiritual Healing

- Although surrounded by friends, family and employees around-the-clock, Elvis is said to have tearfully confessed to hairdresser Larry Geller, "I swear to God, no one knows how lonely I get, and how empty I feel." For a time,

Geller became Elvis' spiritual guru, discussing different philosophies on the meaning of life and introducing him to various spiritual writings, including the book *The Impersonal Life*, which Elvis studied intensely. Inspired by the gardens at Self-Realization Park in Pacific Heights, California, he commissioned what became his "Meditation Garden." He wanted a place to get away and meditate: "some place that's really pretty and peaceful where I could think and be by myself."

A Listening Ear

- In 1969, Elvis added the black female vocal group Sweet Inspiration to his stage show to provide a bit of spicy soul. "I call the Sweet Inspirations my analysts. If anything goes wrong, I go to their dressing room and I close the door and I confess everything to them."

LIFE

Wisdom through Trials

- Elvis experienced extreme opposites in life, from an impoverished childhood of limited possibility to unimagined wealth and iconic success. He was known around the world by his first name, yet was no stranger to the isolation of loneliness. He felt that these experiences gave him a unique empathy with the greater world around him. In 1958, while serving in the army, Elvis received news that his beloved mother Gladys had died of a heart attack. Of that time, he later reflected, "I think that things like that, as tragic as they are, tend to make you a little better human being, because you learn more about yourself. It gives you a better understanding of yourself, as well as other people."

I Am What I Am

- From an early age Elvis had a strong sense of self. He was never swayed by peer pressure or criticism to conform to what others thought he should be. Instead, he dressed, acted, sang and performed to please himself – and it ended up pleasing millions. "I was nobody; a small town kid in a big city, without a dime in my pocket. Not too good in class, kinda shy . . . and the other guys wore GI haircuts. I wanted to be noticed. My hair, the black shirt and pants I wore did it. But don't think I didn't take a lot of kidding from my friends. Still, I stuck with it. I guess I always knew if you want to stand out in a crowd, you gotta be different."

It's a Sin to Tell a Lie

- "Don't be like nobody else or you'll be livin' a lie, and that ain't livin'."

Right and Wrong

- "I think I know right from wrong. In other words, you have to be careful out in the world. It's easy to get trapped into something, it's so easy."

Honesty Is the Best Policy

- In 1956, an interviewer commended Elvis for being very truthful and frank. He thought, aside from his music, one reason that fans liked Elvis so much was because of his openness and honesty with them. "I feel that you have to," Elvis replied, "because if you lie about something, or if you fake it, it will come back to you. The truth will come out sooner or later and the only thing you've [done] is make an idiot of yourself. So it's best just to come clean from the beginning."

Drinking

- Vernon and Gladys Presley both abused alcohol, as did some in Elvis' entourage. Elvis was proud of the fact that he did not. "Everything in moderation," he said of alcohol, "but it's an enemy. It can ruin lives."

The Simple Life

- "In a lot of the mail I get, people ask questions about the kind of things I do: . . . well I don't smoke and I don't drink, and I like to go to movies."

Seeing the Good in Everything

- Receiving a draft notice just as your career is escalating might have caused some to be angry or even bitter, but not Elvis. His only apprehension was that he feared the public would forget him while he was away for two years. Still, he felt it his duty to serve. In 1960, while in Friedberg, Germany, Elvis was asked if his military experience had been beneficial to him professionally or personally. ". . . Both," he responded. "My career and my personal life. Because I have learned a lot [and] made a lot of friends that I never would have made otherwise." He said there had been, "a lot of good experiences, and some bad ones, naturally. It's good to . . . put yourself to the test . . . What we do here has an effect on America and our way of life . . ."

Memphis Homecoming

- Prior to Elvis' release from the service, it was rumoured that a homecoming celebration was being planned. To nix the idea, Elvis sent a telegram to manager Colonel Parker: "Please convey my thanks to the various groups in Memphis who have suggested a special homecoming for me when I return to Memphis. However, I wish to return to Memphis the same way that any other serviceman returns to his home town, without ceremony or fanfare. I served as they served and was proud to do it. Seeing the city of Memphis, my family, friends and fans will be the most welcome sight in the world to me. I appreciate their kind gesture. I know they will understand, and I am glad you are in agreement with me on this. Best wishes to you and Mrs Parker. From Dad, Grandma and myself." The telegram was instigated by the Colonel and it is speculated that the message was, at least partially, composed by him.

Back in the U.S.A.
- "I've learned one thing in this man's army: Man, coming home is the greatest!"

Kids Just Wanna Have Fun
- Adults critical of Elvis tried to get their communities to ban his shows, but his fans would not be swayed from attending his concerts and having a good time – they packed auditoriums and theatres. "You're not going to stop a group of kids and young people from having a nice time," he pointed out to one interviewer, "because they only grow up once, and they are going to have a ball while they are growing up. I don't blame them and I don't see why anybody else should."

Headline News
- "My daddy once said that the only thing newspapers care about is selling newspapers. I believe that is mostly true."

Life in the Spotlight
- "Your life is not your own, really, because people are gonna want to know what you're doing, where you are, what you wear, what you eat . . . and you have to consider that these people are sincere. They don't know what kind

of life you lead. They don't know what kind of person you are. I try to remember that . . . it's simple, it's no problem, it's no big effort that I put forth."

Sticks and Stones
- In June 1956, *Time* magazine nicknamed Elvis "The Pelvis". The moniker summed up some of the bad press he was receiving about his stage movements. "I don't like them to call me 'Elvis the Pelvis,'" he told a reporter. "It's the most childish expression I've ever heard from an adult: 'Elvis the Pelvis.' But if they want to call me that, there's nothing I can do about it. You just have to accept the good with the bad." A couple of months later, an interviewer asked if he had learned anything from the reviews. "No, I haven't," he said firmly. "Because I don't feel like I'm doing anything wrong."

Just Don't Scare the Kids
- "Anything that don't frighten the children is in good taste, far as I'm concerned."

Do Unto Others
- Female fans often vandalised Elvis' cars, trying to get a piece of something he owned or writing messages with their telephone numbers in lipstick on the paint. Questioned about a recent incident, he told a reporter, "That means nothing to me, sir. That's a car and I've got other cars, but the idea of doing to others what you'd like them to do to you is what's in my craw. It's in the Bible . . . I read my Bible, sir, . . . My Bible tells me that what he sows he will also reap, and if I'm sowing evil and wickedness it will catch up with me. I'm right sure of that, sir, and I don't think I'm bad for people. If I did think I was bad for people, I would go back to driving truck, and I really mean this."

Being Liked

- "It's almost impossible to make everybody like you – you can't please 'em all."

Life After High School

- Proof that life improves after high school: Elvis said, "I never was a lady killer in high school. I had my share of dates, but that's all." Another time he stated, "I wasn't popular in school. I wasn't dating anybody. I failed music – only thing I ever failed. And then they entered me in this talent show, and I came out and did my [first number], 'Till I Waltz Again With You' by Teresa Brewer. And when I came onstage, I heard people kind of rumbling and whispering and so forth, 'cause nobody knew I even sang. It was amazing how popular I became after that. Then I went on through high school and I graduated."

The Green Monster

- "Envy someone an' it pulls you down. Admire them and it builds you up. Which makes more sense?"

Milkcow Boogie

- "Just remember this: Don't go milking the cow on a rainy day. If there's lightning, you may be left holding the bag."

Diet and Exercise

- "The only exercise I get is on the stage." With all the moving Elvis did performing, it was enough to keep him fit – at least in the early part of his career. Several years later, when asked about dieting, he said, "I try to use a little will power . . . because, in this business, especially in the movies . . . weight can be very bad for you."

Temper Tantrums

- "I have a bad temper – extremely bad temper – so much to

the point that I have no idea what I'm doing. I can probably count the times [I've lost my temper], but when I have, it's always pretty bad," Elvis admitted. There are many stories of his losing his temper and later feeling remorse. In the early 1950s, he often played billiards at Southern Bowling Lanes. Realising he'd been hustled in a game, he angrily threw a cue stick and broke it. The manager threw him out and told him he could only return if he paid for the damaged stick and behaved in the future. Days later, Elvis apologetically returned with a new cue stick. On another occasion, he hurled an ashtray at a jukebox that was playing a song he didn't like. The next day he replaced it. In later years he offered gifts, such a jewellery and furs, with his apology. ". . . it doesn't happen very often . . . then I don't like myself, you know, later."

While I Was Sleeping
- Describing some of his nightmares, Elvis shared, "I dream I'm about to fight somebody or about to be in a car wreck, or that I'm breaking things."

Keeping Things Lively
- Elvis possessed a sometimes lethal combination of excessive energy, short attention span and quick temper. Once, while eating a cheeseburger and watching television, a haemorrhoid commercial came on, talking about itching and burning. Elvis threw his cheeseburger at the screen, then grabbed one of his guns and shot a bullet through it. Another time, he shot up a television set and chandelier in a hotel where he was staying, then wrote out a check for the damages. Of his temper, he once said, "I'd rather be angry than bored."

T-R-O-U-B-L-E

- "The only kind of trouble I ever been in was stealing eggs when I was real little."

A Man Is as Good as His Word

- When Elvis signed with Colonel Parker for management, he promised to be loyal. Early in Elvis' career, in 1955, he sent Colonel Parker a telegram: "Dear Colonel, Words can never tell you how my folks and I appreciate what you did for me. I've always known, and now my folks are assured, that you are the best, most wonderful person I could ever hope to work with. Believe me when I say I will stick with you through thick and thin, and do everything I can to uphold your faith in me. Again, I say thanks and I love you like a father. Elvis Presley." One reason Elvis remained working with Colonel Parker, through disagreements and the Colonel's greedy deals, was that he believed in honouring an obligation. "You don't go back on them," Elvis once said of promises. "You just don't. All it takes is to do it once, and you've lost folks' trust forever." Whenever Elvis and the Colonel had disagreements regarding his career or the Colonel's business deals, the master manipulator reminded Elvis of his promise and Elvis always acquiesced.

Keeping it Real

- Wealth, fame and adulation seemed to come upon Elvis almost overnight, yet he never lost sight of whom he was and where he came from. An interviewer once asked him what he thought of himself. Elvis responded in a humble, yet profound way, ". . . as a human being who has been extremely fortunate in so many ways."

Eyes Are the Mirror of the Soul

- "A person's eyes tell you more than their words."

Room for Improvement

- Even at the peak of his popularity, Elvis still strove to progress. "I have a lot that I would like to do, that I would like to accomplish." Not one to be complacent about his success, he wanted to improve both as an actor and as a recording artist: "I try to get better songs and sing a little better."

His Hand in Mine

- "God gave me my voice. If I ever turned my back on Him, I'd be finished."

Talking to God

- "Sometimes it's good to get a few words out . . ." Elvis said of prayer, ". . . just to put yourself on your knees."

It's All Been Good

- "Thank God, I have been pretty fortunate. I haven't made any, you know, bad decisions."

People Are People

- A rumour circulated that Elvis had said, "The only thing Negroes can do for me is buy my records and shine my shoes." It purported that he made the statement in either Boston, a city he had never visited, or on Edward R. Murrow's television show, which he had never appeared on. To anyone who knew Elvis, the accusation was outrageous. In his youth, Elvis had often attended black church services because he enjoyed the music, and he was friends with several black musicians. Finally, *Jet* magazine sent reporter Louie Robinson to the set of *Jailhouse Rock* to get the truth. "I never said anything like that," Elvis said emphatically. "People who know me, know I wouldn't have said it." After confronting Elvis, Robinson also spoke with a few people who did know Elvis well. Satisfied the statement had been falsely credited, Robinson wrote, "To Elvis, people are people, regardless of race, colour or creed." After Ivory Joe Hunter visited Elvis at Graceland, he stated, "He showed me every courtesy and I think he's one of the greatest."

Passing Judgment

- Borrowing from the song, "Walk A Mile In My Shoes," Elvis often said, "Don't criticise what you don't understand, son. You never walked in that man's shoes."

Money Honey

- "Sharing money is what gives it its value."

The Ripple Effect

- Both Vernon, who oversaw Elvis' finances, and the Colonel, often berated Elvis for his spending habits, particularly his impulsive buying sprees. But Elvis would not be swayed. He was big-hearted and extremely generous, bestowing cars, jewellery and other expensive gifts on friends and acquaintances. While shopping for a new car, he thought nothing of buying one for everyone else in the dealership at the time. If someone admired a piece of jewellery or clothing he wore, he might take if off and give it to them. In 1971, he gave his favourite waitress at the Formosa Café in Hollywood a Cadillac El Dorado. While shopping for a new car for himself, he noticed Minnie L. Person, a black bank teller, window shopping. He invited her inside and asked which automobile was the car of her dreams. She selected the El Dorado. Elvis handed her the keys and said, "Happy Birthday – the Cadillac is yours." He loved seeing the joy on the faces of those he surprised with his generous and extravagant gifts. "It's like throwing a stone in a pond," he said, "it ripples out."

Why Am I Here and Where Am I Going?

- Larry Geller was a last-minute replacement for Elvis' regular hairdresser. At their first meeting, the two struck up a conversation that led to a discussion of the meaning of life. Elvis soon became consumed with the study of philosophy and spiritual writing. He told Geller, "I've always known that there had to be a purpose for my life. I mean, there's got to be a reason . . . why I was chosen to be Elvis Presley."

Your Own Compass

- "Do what's right for you, as long as it don't hurt no one."

Music and Religion

- "Religion is like music: You experience them and they both move you."

Saints and Sinners

- Elvis was an active member of the Assembly of God church in his youth. When he began touring, he attended far less frequently. Still, he always professed a faith in God and tried to live in a way that would never bring shame to his parents or God. "I ain't no saint, but I've tried never to do anything that would hurt my family or offend God," Elvis told a Memphis reporter in the 1950s. "I figure all any kid needs is hope and the feeling he or she belongs. If I could do or say anything that would give some kid that feeling, I would believe I had contributed something to the world."

A Little Understanding

- "What becomes important as you get older is understanding . . . instead of worrying about the things you can't do anymore."

Dr Presley

• Few people knew that Elvis considered entering the medical field. During a 1962 interview with Lloyd Shearer, he spoke of his continued interest in medicine: "I keep up with modern medicine, medical science, medical discoveries, different diseases – nobody knows that. I've been doing it for a long, long time. I get doctor's handbooks, PDR – which is a *Physicians Desk Reference* – and it's pretty interesting . . . At one time, when I got out of school, I thought I wanted to be a doctor or something in the medical profession. That's what I thought I wanted to be, but I didn't have the money to go to college . . ."

Seek Ye Out of the Best Books

• A hectic schedule left Elvis with precious few moments for personal reflection, yet he found encouragement in the inspirational thoughts of others. "I read a lot of philosophy, some poetry. Have you ever heard of a book called *Leaves of Gold*? It's by [several] different people. It's different people's philosophies on life and death, and everything else. That [type of writing] interests me – to get to read different people's opinions on different things." [*Leaves of Gold: An Anthology of Prayers, Memorable Phrases, Inspirational Verse, and Prose*, by Clyde Francis Lytle (Editor), Brownlow Publishing Company, 1995.]

Everybody's A Critic

• "I was telling a reporter a little earlier today . . . regardless of who you are or what you do, there's gonna be people that don't like you. There were people that didn't like Jesus Christ – they killed him – and Jesus Christ was a perfect man. There's gonna be people that don't like you, regardless of who you are or what you do. Because if everybody thought the same way, they'd be driving the same car, they'd be marrying the same woman, and that wouldn't work out . . ."

Fool, Fool, Fool

- "You can't fool yourself or the public for very long."

Judgment Day

- "I just wish the people would stop judging a tree by its bark," Elvis said of those who pronounced his stage show vulgar. "They should come out to the show and judge it by themselves," he said, instead of by "something they have heard or something they have read."

The King

- Uncomfortable with his latest nickname, "The King", Elvis told a reporter, "I'm not a king. Christ is King. I'm just a singer."

Baby Talk

- "Only babies call people names."

Viva Las Vegas

- "Man, I really like Vegas," Elvis enthusiastically told a Memphis reporter, shortly after his first run of shows there. "I'm going back there the first chance I get." Las Vegas appealed to Elvis because it was open 24-hours-a-day, providing company during the long nights when he couldn't sleep. Showgirls fawned over him and he created a hullabaloo wherever he went. But he never drank and he did not gamble. "It don't appeal to me. [I] never dropped a nickel in a slot machine."

Beginner's Luck

- "If you're willing to accept good luck, you have to be willing to accept some bad luck too."

No Regrets

- "You can't stay on top forever," Elvis told a reporter who asked what he would do if his popularity declined. "Even if I stopped singing tomorrow, I'd have no regrets. I had a ball while I was there."

Have A Happy

- If you could have anything, what would it be? "It's a magical question," Elvis responded. "I suppose the most important thing in a person's life is happiness. Not the worldly things . . . you can have cars, you can have money, you can have a fabulous home – you can have everything. But if you're not happy, what have you got? So I suppose that if I can just continue to make other people's life enjoyable, and to make my own life happy, well then, that's all I could expect out of life."

Evils, Lives and Elvis

- Throughout his career, Elvis was accused of being nasty, vulgar and downright evil. He took it all in stride. In fact, the bad press made him all the more popular with concert ticket and recording buying youth. In a 1969 interview he joked, "My name's got 'evils' and 'lives'. It's probably better not to wonder too much about it."

Life Is Not A Dress Rehearsal

- Elvis understood the importance of living in the moment: ". . . you only pass through life once, Jack; you don't come back for an encore." Each day was a gift to be savoured.

Life

- "Do something worth remembering."

This Is The Story

- "I did the best I could." What better punctuation to a life, than to have put forth your best effort.

Clear Conscience

- "I've examined my conscience and asked myself if I led anybody astray, even indirectly, and I'm at peace with my conscience."

'Til We Meet Again

- At the close of a concert on his final tour in 1977, Elvis told the audience, " 'Til we meet you again, may God bless you. Adios."

LOVE

The Ideal Woman

- In a last press conference before Private Elvis set sail for his army assignment in Germany, he was asked to describe the ideal girl: "Female, sir!" he responded.

I Don't Bite

- At a Tampa, Florida performance on August 5, 1956, an adoring fan came backstage to interview Elvis for a high school newspaper. The girl was so nervous she had difficulty asking her questions. Elvis tried to calm her with humour, "Don't be so nervous, I'm not gonna bite you." Finally, she asked if he was looking for a girl. He quickly responded, "I think I found her – you!"

Don't It Make You Wanna Go Home

- "I was raised in a pretty decent home and everything. My folks always made me behave, whether I wanted to or not." Regardless of their sometimes desperate circumstances, Gladys insisted Elvis learn courtesy and respect for others. "I always had to be polite and do the right things.

My folks were real strict. I rebelled sometimes, but I guess their strictness was the best thing that ever happened to me, even if I didn't realise it. My mom and dad loved me too much ever to spoil me, even though I was an only child."

Mother's Day

- Elvis set an example of love and respect for mothers in honouring his own mother, Gladys. "You must be true to yourself. But above all . . . you must honour and love your mother." He further showed his respect for all mothers by recording special Mother's Day radio broadcasts beginning in 1965. On Mother's Day, 1973, he performed a special matinee show at the Sahara Hotel at Lake Tahoe, Nevada, with proceeds being donated to a local hospital.

Ladies and Gentlemen

- "Women should be treated like ladies."

Pet Names

- "Satnin" was the name of affection Elvis bestowed on his mother and later gave his wife, Priscilla. After his fraternal grandmother, Minnie Mae, successfully dodged a ball thrown at her, he dubbed her "Dodger", and ever after the name stuck. Of nicknames he said, "They're real powerful; they can hurt or thy can tie you to people in an affectionate way."

Goose Bumps

- Attempting to articulate what it felt like when he was onstage, Elvis told girlfriend June Juanico, "I don't know; it's had to explain. It's like your whole body gets goose bumps, but it's not goose bumps. It's not a chill, either. It's like a surge of electricity going through you. It's almost like making love, but it's even stronger than that."

Love of Music

- Music was always in and around the Presley home. Vernon Presley had a good voice. He and Elvis enjoyed singing gospel songs like "Amazing Grace" and "Precious Love" together. Elvis loved all styles of music and particularly enjoyed the gospel music he heard in church. "My mother and dad both love to sing," he said. "They tell me when I was three or four I got away from them in church and I walked up in front of the choir and started beating time."

Gospel Music

- "Gospel music is the purest thing there is on this earth."

The Most Eligible Bachelor

- The press loved speculating about Elvis' romances. In the summer of 1956, the story was that he had proposed to June Juanico, who he had recently seen a few times. Hearing the rumour on WNOE Radio in New Orleans, Elvis made a surprise stop at the station. "I was in Biloxi and I heard on the radio that I was supposed to be engaged to somebody, so I came down here to see who I was supposed to be engaged to." The disc jockey jumped on the opportunity to ask if Elvis was serious about any girl. "No," he responded, "I am not. I'm serious about my career." Over the next few months, Elvis continued to see Juanico. The following June, she married someone else.

I Love Paris in the Springtime

- On at least two occasions, Elvis spent his army leave time in Paris. "I was in Paris twice," he told AFN Radio interviewer, Johnny Paris. "Once for 10 days and another time for six." He punctuated what he remembered most with a whistle and added, "Well, I'll tell you: it's a gay time, if you like night life."

Is This Love?

- "Well, as you're growing up, a lot of times you think you're in love with someone, and then later on in your life you find out that you're wrong. Actually, you didn't love them, you only thought you did. And I was no different. Several times as I was growing up I would have probably married, and my mother and dad talked to me and told me, 'You better wait and find out that this is just what you want,' and I'm glad that I did." Elvis met Priscilla in 1959 and they married eight years later. Although the couple later divorced, it was Elvis' only marriage. The two remained friends and there was an enduring love between them.

I'll Never Let You Go (Little Darlin')

- "No matter what our problems might be . . . I'll never divorce Priscilla." Never say never.

Puppy Love

- When he was growing up, Elvis said of girlfriends, "I had a lot of puppy love." A few months later, in August 1956, when pressed further with the question, had he ever been in love, Elvis explained, "I thought I was when I was growing up. But I wasn't. You know, when you're growing up, you sometimes think you're in love. You sometimes think that this is it – that you'll never find another one . . . but then you grow up and you laugh at yourself."

The Perfect Girl

- Asked what kind of girls Elvis liked, his honest response was, "A lot of different types – actresses and schoolgirls."

The Thrill of Your Love

- When asked if women were one of his hobbies, Elvis responded with a laugh, "Well, I couldn't call them a hobby – it's more like a pastime!"

A Date with the King

- No question about it, Elvis loved women – and they loved him. He never lacked female companionship, sometimes seeing several girls in one day – or night. "I love going out on dates," Elvis shared while taping *The Truth About Me* in 1956, "especially with a girl that likes to have fun – the kind of fun I mean is, just going out and looking around places and things; wondering about people and trying to win prizes at the amusement parks, and just generally having a good time." Asked if there was a special girl, he responded, "I date a few different ones, but nobody in particular . . . I've never dated a girl three years – I've never dated one three months."

Dating

- "I haven't given marriage much thought. I like to date girls who are fun to be with."

I Got a Woman

- "She [Priscilla] has everything a man could want in a wife. If she's not the right girl, then there just isn't one."

True Love

- Of marriage, Elvis once advised: "Wait. Wait and find out if this person is really what you want. True love will survive the wait." Elvis did wait, eight years to be exact, and his love did survive. For a time. He first met his future wife, 14-year-old Priscilla Beaulieu, on 13 July 1959. Though 10 years her senior, there was an immediate attraction between them. Elvis later told a friend that Priscilla was "like the woman I've been looking for all my life." The couple married on May 1, 1967.

Pretty Girls

- "I love the fans. I love the pretty girls. When they come running to me, I want to run to them, not away from them. I hope they don't blame me when army regulations force me to look straight ahead on duty. I want them to know I'm not ignoring them."

Chasing Elvis

- Women routinely made passes at Elvis and he rarely turned them down. The press frequently linked Elvis to different women and rumoured that he was engaged to be married. When he appeared in Canada in early 1957, interviewer Mac Lipson asked about his plans for marriage and how he felt about girls chasing after him. "I have no plans for getting married," he said. "If the girl is on the chase for that, then she's on a wild goose chase, because I can usually sense whether or not that's what they're after or not."

Girls! Girls! Girls!

- Colonel Parker became increasingly agitated over the scandalous press Elvis had received in connection with his relationship with June Juanico. Several times Parker told Elvis he had to do something about it. After June gave an unauthorised (by the Colonel) interview recounting their "courtship", Elvis told the press: "Now this is the way it is: I got 25 girls I date regular. She's just one of the girls." Later that night, as June travelled with Elvis to the next gig, he put a cigar in his mouth and imitated Parker saying, "You're seeing too much of this girl from Biloxi. She's not good for you, son. You can't be linked to any one girl."

Because of Love

- "Girl fans would throw their handkerchiefs at me and I'd

blow my nose on 'em and toss 'em right back, and them ladies would hug their hankies to their breasts and never wash 'em . . . that's devotion."

Balancing Marriage and Career

- "It's hard to put the two, marriage and the career, together . . . it's best to be honest up front, which is more important to you." This may be one reason the relationship between Elvis and *Viva Las Vegas* co-star Ann-Margret never became more than a fling. When Priscilla asked Elvis about the actress, he described her as "a typical Hollywood starlet," then reassured Priscilla by adding, "into their careers, and their man comes second. I don't want to be second to anything or anyone. That's why you don't have to worry about my falling in love with my so-called leading ladies." Though he clearly wanted someone who put him first in their life, he was not willing to make the same commitment.

Flip, Flop and Fly

- Women of all ages swooned for Elvis. The lyrics to his song, Flip, Flop and Fly, could not have been more aptly written: "I'm like a Mississippi bullfrog, sittin' on a hollow stump, I got so many women, I don't know which way to jump."

Career, Love and Marriage

- In September 1957, Elvis gave an interview in Portland, Oregon where he was quoted as saying, "There's nothing more important than love and marriage. I do think that marriage would hurt my career now, though." He had not yet met the love of his life, Priscilla Beaulieu. It would be another 10 years before he married.

Young and Beautiful

- "Guys, I've just met the prettiest girl I've ever seen. Her name is Priscilla. Someday I'll probably marry her." And he did.

I Want You, I Need You, I Love You

- "We decided to get married about six months ago. Priscilla was one of the few girls who was interested in me for me alone. We never discussed marriage in Germany, we just met at her father's house, went to the movies and did a lot of driving, that's all. I waited for her to grow up."

One-Sided Love Affair

- Newspapers carried the headline, "Elvis Wins Love of Ann-Margret", reporting they were engaged. Elvis was furious that A-M would lie to the press about their relationship. Priscilla was obviously deeply hurt – she was, after all, living at Graceland with the promise that Elvis would marry her. She hurled a flower vase across the room. Elvis grabbed her and exclaimed, "I didn't know this was going to get out of hand. I want a woman who's going to understand that things like this might just happen. Are you going to be her – or not?"

No Comparison

- "I don't compare my girlfriends with my mother." Interestingly, Elvis nicknamed girlfriend June Juanico and later girlfriend/wife Priscilla Presley, "Satnin" – the same pet-name he had given his mother Gladys.

The Girl of His Dreams

- Shortly after Elvis was discharged from the military and returned to Memphis, he held a press conference, during which he was asked about Priscilla. Though he had found the girl of his dreams, she was a teenager and 10 years his junior. Elvis knew how the press coverage surrounding Jerry Lee Lewis's marriage to his 14-year-old cousin had destroyed his career, and Elvis would not make the same mistake. He responded to the questions about a budding romance by saying, "In Germany I met a girl I really cared for, the most beautiful creature I've ever seen in my life. She was only 16 [she was actually 14] but grown up and mature and my Colonel's daughter. She's from a very good family . . ."

Desire

- Priscilla and Elvis wed almost four years after she moved into Graceland. After she was living at the mansion, she pressed Elvis to consummate their relationship – but he insisted they wait until after they were married. "I want it to be something to look forward to," he told her. "It keeps the desire there." Elvis later confessed, in detail, to Priscilla what the relationship between he and Ann-Margret had been. It was Priscilla he loved, would later marry, and have a child with.

Just Teasing

- "I could make you like me if I tried," Elvis flirtingly told a female reporter on the set of his picture *Love Me Tender.* "I'm just teasin' now, but I'd be sweet, and you'd like me because I was sweet, wouldn't you?"

The Cost of Love

- "I learned young that havin' a girlfriend was about the most expensive thing there is – besides havin' a wife."

God's Love Felt through Music

- "Church was our way of life since I can remember," Elvis told movie columnist May Mann. "The last time I went, there was so much confusion and autograph seeking that out of respect, I've stayed away." He had, however, undertaken a spiritual quest for the meaning of life with Larry Geller. The long-considered idea of making a gospel record resurfaced. "I've been working on religious songs for an album. I feel God and his goodness, and I believe I can express his love for us in music."

Known Only to Him

- "My first love is spiritual music – some of the old coloured spirituals from way back. I know practically every religious song that's ever been written."

Rock'n'Roll Wedding

- Colonel Parker made all the arrangements for Elvis and Priscilla's May 1, 1967 nuptials. Held at the Aladdin Hotel in Las Vegas, the wedding was neither sacred, nor private. Instead, the Colonel staged a publicity event, even inviting the press to the reception. Years earlier, Elvis had predicted, "I'll fall in love someday and maybe there'll be a rock'n'roll wedding." He got what he wished for.

Stand By Your Man

- In 1972, Elvis said: "What I expect is for a woman to stand by her man . . . not sleep around or cuss." However, he was not willing to give the same in return.

Love, Elvis

- When Priscilla informed Elvis of her intention to divorce him, it was a devastating blow to his heart and ego. The King of Rock'n'Roll had millions of women, including beautiful movie stars, chasing after him, and yet his own wife wanted to leave him. Eventually, the two worked through a divorce settlement and even left the courthouse holding hands. Of their divorce announcement he said, it was a "sad thing" and that "you can still love someone and be wrong for them." There remained a love and bond between them that could not be broken. "We are the best of friends," he later stated, "and always have been. Our divorce came about not because of another man, but because of circumstances involving my career, nothing else. Regardless of what you have read or have been led to believe. I don't think it was fair on Priscilla, with me gone so often and travelling so much." When Priscilla and a friend opened Bis and Beau's, an upscale boutique in Beverly Hills, Elvis sent her pink rosebuds to celebrate the opening, with a note that read, "Good luck on your venture. Love, Elvis."

Love Me, Love the Life I Lead

- "Dogs love you no matter how much you do or don't have. You can count on them more than you can count on most people – they don't leave you like some people do."

Self Love

- Did Elvis like himself? That was the question Lloyd Shearer put to him in a 1962 interview. "Sometimes," he laughed. "What I mean by liking myself, I'm proud of the way I was brought up to believe and to treat people and have respect for people. I am pleased to a certain point."

For the Love of Jell-o!

- When the King was asked to name his favourite foods, he responded: "I like pork chops, country ham, creamed potatoes . . . I eat a lot of Jell-o – fruit Jell-o."

It's Only Love

- "Love and warmth – that's what everyone is looking for."

SUCCESS

Courage and Success

- Unable to accompany himself and finding no one to assist him, 10-year-old Elvis entered a 1945 Mississippi–Alabama Fair talent competition, singing "Old Shep" a cappella. "I didn't have any music or anything and I couldn't get anybody to play for me. And I couldn't play for myself, because I didn't know how. So I just went out there and started singing. I'd set my heart on singing and nothing in the world could have stopped me from entering the talent contest. I did it all by my own." He placed fifth.

School Days

- "I would lie awake wondering what I was going to do. I really wasn't much good at anything. At school I'd been only an average student. I mean I didn't flunk, but I didn't do too good, either. I couldn't figure out how I was ever going to make something out of myself."

Dare to Dream

- Mississippi: his father drifting from job to job, while his mother laboured as a cotton picker. From this impoverished childhood, Elvis had the vision to dream of a better life: "When I was a child . . ." he recalled, "I was a dreamer. I read comic books, and I was the hero of the comic book. I saw movies, and I was the hero in the movie. So every dream I ever dreamed has come true a hundred times . . . I learned very early in life that: 'Without a song, the day would never end; without a song, a man ain't got a friend; without a song, the road would never bend – without a song.' So I keep singing a song. Goodnight. Thank you." (Elvis quotes lyrics from "Without A Song")

The Man Who Rejected Elvis

- Eddie Bond will forever be known as the man who told Elvis to continue driving a truck "because you're never going to make it as a singer." In 1954, Elvis auditioned to be a singer in one of Eddie's two bands that played in the Memphis area. Of the rejection, Elvis later recalled, "I wonder what Eddie Bond thinks now. Man, that sonofabitch broke my heart."

The First Time

- In the summer of 1953, Elvis walked into Sam Phillips' Memphis Recording Service to make a record. He recorded two songs, 'My Happiness' and 'That's When Your Heartache Begins', in one attempt and took the original pressing. "I didn't have enough money to do the record over, so I decided to let it stand as it was. I figured, if nobody else liked the thing, mom would, anyway; and she did." Elvis was tickled to hear his voice and Gladys loved it – they played the recording over and over until they nearly wore it out. Years later, Elvis told interviewers, "We still got the record at home. It's so thin that we can't play it."

Like Nobody Else

- "I don't sound like nobody," Elvis answered, when Marion Keisker at Sun Records asked who he sounded like. From the beginning, Elvis knew he was unique. He wasn't copying or adapting someone else's style, he was creating a new sound and technique. He was an original that didn't sound or perform like anybody else.

Overnight Sensation

- "I was an overnight sensation. A year after they heard me the first time, they called me back!" Elvis made his first recording at Sam Phillips's recording studio in the summer of 1953. He paid for the session himself and gave the recording to his mother as a gift. Though it was just as much a gift for himself – "I'd really wanted to hear myself sing. I can't remember exactly what hit me that day, but I had to know what my voice sounded like." Leaving the recording studio Elvis gave his name and telephone number to office manager, Marian Keisker, offering to sing demos. "That same company called me about a year later and said, 'We've got a song that you might be able to do.' It was 12 o'clock, and they [asked] 'Can you be here about 3 o'clock?' I was there by the time they hung up the phone!"

Super Elvis
- "When I was a boy, I was the hero in comic books and movies. I grew up believing in a dream. Now, I've lived it out. That's all a man can ask for."

My Wish Came True
- In April 1953, Elvis began driving a delivery truck for Crown Electric. The job afforded him time to daydream: "When I was driving my truck, and one of them big shiny cars went by, it started me to daydreaming. I always felt that someday, somehow, something would change for me. I didn't know exactly what, but it was a feeling that the future looked kinda bright." Two months later, in late June, Sam Phillips booked Elvis to record 'Without You' at Sun Records. Although the song was not right for Elvis' voice and style, it was the beginning of his dream coming true.

Gifts from God
- "I believe in the Bible. I believe that all good things come

from God. I don't believe I'd sing the way I do if God
hadn't wanted me to."

An Auspicious Beginning

- "The reason we couldn't get anything was that I was
  scared," Elvis said of his first recording session, "and when
  you're scared, you can't breathe right. And besides, the
  song weren't my kind of thing." Sam Phillips was not
  impressed with Elvis' rendering of 'Without You'. But he
  must have heard something worth pursuing, because he
  called guitarist Scott Moore and bassist Bill Black and
  asked them to work with Elvis. Within three weeks they
  had recorded 'That's All Right Mama' and 'Blue Moon of
  Kentucky', Elvis' first single.

A Natural

- "I never did sing in public in my life, until I made these
  first records."

A First Time for Everything

- "[The] first time I appeared on stage, it scared me to
  death!" Elvis later recalled of his first major concert, on
  July 30, 1954 at the Overton Park Shell in Memphis. "I
  really didn't know what the yelling was about. I didn't
  realise that my body was moving. It was a natural thing to
  me. So to the manager backstage I said, 'What'd I do?
  What'd I do?' He said, 'Well, whatever it was, go back and
  do it again!'" The crowd cheered him back onstage. In
  another interview, he said, "I went back out for an encore,
  and I did a little more, and the more I did, the wilder they
  went."

Sideburns Are the Best Form of Flattery

- People were curious about everything Elvis did. Many a
  reporter asked about his inspiration to grow sideburns.

"How I happened to wear sideburns was, my dad was a truck driver and I admired him and other truck drivers I knew. Most wore sideburns and moustaches. So when I was 16, I grew sideburns to look as much like them as possible."

Dressed for Success

- A stunning dresser, Elvis loved clothes. Long before his music career took off, he frequented Lansky Brothers' shop on Beale Street in Memphis. He once promised owners Bernard and Guy Lansky, "When I have me some money, I'm gonna come in and buy you out," which he nearly did over the years. Even in his leisure time, Elvis dressed in beautiful silk shirts and trousers, never jeans. They were a reminder of his impoverished childhood. In 1976, when a Las Vegas dresser handed him a pair of blue denim overalls, he responded, "Honey, I left those in Mississippi 200 years ago. Honey, I can't put them on. You've got to be kiddin' me." Of his dress, he said, "On the street," he preferred "real conservative clothes, but on stage I like them as flashy as you can get 'em."

Give Them Something to Talk About

- The first time Elvis performed on stage, he was so nervous his legs wiggled – and the audience went wild. "Everybody was hollering and I didn't know what they were hollering at . . . My manager told me . . . they were hollering because I was wiggling my legs, and I was unaware . . . so I went back out for an encore and I did a little more." And they loved it. "You have to put on a show for people. People can buy your records and hear you sing, but . . . you have to put on a show in order to draw a crowd. If I just stood out there and sang, and never moved a muscle, the people would say, 'My goodness, I can stay home and list to his records.' You have to give them a show – somethin' to talk about." It was important to Elvis that his fans, who spent hard-earned money for his concert tickets, got their money's worth.

Thrill of Your Love

- Arguably, no rock'n'roll or movie star signed more auto-graphs than Elvis. He hated to turn anyone away. He loved having contact with his fans. But as crowds grew bigger, he had to employ body guards to protect himself from being hurt by overly aggressive fans. "If it wasn't for getting mobbed, maybe clothes torn off – stuff like that – I would go right out in the middle of those people. I hate to turn anybody down who wants an autograph, who buys pictures and wants to get 'em signed."

The Shirt Off His Back

- "I don't mind if the fans rip the shirt from my back – they put it there."

Here Today, Gone Tomorrow

- Girls went crazy over Elvis and even he could not explain it. "I guess it's just something God gave me. I believe that . . . and I'm grateful. Only, I'm afraid. I'm afraid I'll go out like a light, just like I came on."

Defending His Fans

- Frequently criticised in the media, Elvis seemed to not let it bother him. But attack his fans and he took offence. When Elvis heard a scathing review of one of his shows, where the critic not only blasted him, but called his fans "idiots", he defensively responded: "Sir, those kids that come here and pay their money to see this show come to have a good time. I mean, I'm not running Mr Rau down, but I just don't see that he should call those people idiots – because they're somebody's kids. They're somebody's decent kids, probably that was raised in a decent home, and he hasn't got any right to call those kids idiots. If they want to pay their money to come out and jump around and scream and yell – it's their business. They'll grow up someday and grow out of that. While they're young, let them have their fun. Don't call them a bunch of idiots, because they're just human beings like he is."

Having a Ball

- Asked what he thought of his fans' near-hysterical response to his performances, Elvis responded simply, "They're just teenagers having a ball." He loved the attention of his fans. Another time he said, "I really enjoy it. I think it's real great that they feel that much about [me], you know. I've had people ask me, 'Do you think it is silly?' I do not. I think it's wonderful. I'm glad that they think enough of me . . . They have given me the most wonderful time in my life."

Excuse Me

- "I'll bet I could burp and make them squeal." And he did.

All Press Is Good Press

- No other artist generated the press that Elvis did. The more they criticised him, the bigger the headline; the bigger the headline and controversy, the more they talked about him – and more and more youth flocked to his concerts, bought his records and went to the theatre to see his films. "Sometimes every knock can be a boost. When everybody agrees on something and someone says, 'I like that,' they start talking about something else. When there's no controversy, there's no news. When they quit talking about you, you're dead."

Just a Regular Guy

- "I don't know what all the fuss is about. I'm just a guy who makes music – no different from anybody else."

Waiting on Elvis

- Teens waited outside hotels, recording studios, stage doors – any place that Elvis might be, hoping for a chance to see him and maybe get an autograph or picture. In Portland, Oregon, an interviewer asked the incredulous question: Did he mind teenagers waiting to see him? "I don't mind it. In fact, if you come to play and nobody's there to meet you, you start wondering."

The Power of the People

- Of his success, Elvis said, "I owe it, mainly, to the people."

Make Believe

- Asked how he felt about his rapid rise to success, Elvis said, "It all happened so fast that I didn't hardly have time to think about it . . . I just kept going . . . I can't even think about it . . . it might be all over, and then I'd be back driving a truck." When asked the same question a year later, in 1956, he exclaimed, "It feels pretty good. It all happened so fast . . . I'm afraid to wake up; afraid it's liable to be a dream."

Stage Fright

- Watching Elvis' dynamite performance, it is hard to believe he ever experienced stage fright; he always appeared so confident. "I've been in front of a lot of audiences, but

I always get nervous," he admitted, ". . . after the first couple of songs I feel okay . . . I always go out with the thought in my mind, 'Are they going to like me? Are they going to throw rocks at me or something like that?'"

Developing Talents

- Everyone is blessed with gifts and abilities; Elvis perceived his to be an average talent: "I'm not kidding myself," he once explained. "My voice alone is just an ordinary voice." What was extraordinary about Elvis was his ability to realise his strengths and to use them to compensate areas he thought he was lacking in. "If I stand still while I'm singing, I'm dead, man. I might as well go back to driving a truck." Would Elvis have been Elvis if he just stood at the mike and sang?

Singing Gospel

- Gospel music was always a part of Elvis' life. It was the music he heard in the Assembly of God church where his family worshiped and in the all–black churches he sneaked into to hear their choirs sing. "Gospel music is the purest thing there is on this earth," he said. While playing in Las Vegas, Elvis, his band and entourage would wind down after a concert with an informal jam session of gospel music. "We do two shows a night for five weeks. A lotta times we'll go upstairs and sing until daylight – gospel songs. We grew up with it . . . it more or less puts your mind at ease. It does mine." In 1960, he released his first all gospel album, *His Hand In Mine*. A few years later, in 1967, he released *How Great Thou Art*, another collection of gospel songs. By year's end, the beautiful renditions of the music Elvis loved brought him his first Grammy Award for Best Sacred Performance.

That's the Way it Is

- "When you're a celebrity, people treat you nicer. The bad part is, they also tell you what they think you want to hear, which ain't always the truth."

I Heard It on the Radio

- Frequently, Elvis found himself in the centre of rumours about his personal life. Many involved women he was supposed to be dating, engaged, or married to. "If I were to decide to get married . . . it wouldn't be a secret," Elvis said in 1956. "I'd let everybody know about it. But I have no plans for marriage. I have no specific loves and I'm not engaged. I'm not going steady with anybody . . . I don't know how it got started, but everywhere I go . . . [I hear] I'm engaged, or married, or I've got four or five kids." A day later, another disc jockey asked about the rumour that Elvis was paid a buck a minute for an interview. "That's one of the most untrue rumours that I've heard yet," he responded. A couple of weeks earlier, he dismissed the rumour that he had shot his mother: "Well," he laughed, "I think that would take the cake – that's about the farthest one I've ever heard." Many would have been angry at the press, but not Elvis. When interviewer Hy Gardner asked if Elvis felt any animosity toward reporters, he said, "Not really. Those people have a job to do and they do it."

Gossip Central

- Frequently the target of tabloid journalism and gossip, Elvis put it quite simply, "Little talk for little minds."

Defending the Faith

- In 1956, interviewer Paul Wilder referred to an article that misquoted Elvis as using the term 'Holy Roller'. But Elvis quickly cut him off stating firmly "I have *never* used that expression! . . . I belong to an Assembly of God church, which is a holiness church . . . and some character called them 'Holy Rollers' – that's where that got started. I always attended a church where people sang – where people stood up and sang in the choir and worshiped God, you know. I have never used the expression 'Holy Roller'." Trying again to create controversy, Wilder asked if there was peppy music at Elvis' church services. "Peppy music?" he repeated incredulously. "They sing hymns and spirituals – they sing spiritual songs."

A Little Knowledge Is a Dangerous Thing

- Often self-deprecating, Elvis commented of his talent, "I don't know anything about music. In my line you don't have to."

Public Eyes

- "Anybody that's in the public eye, their life is never private. Everything you do, the public knows about it; and that's the way it's always been and always will be."

Cadillac Man

- "When I was a kid, I'd sit on our porch and watch those long, low cars whiz by. I told myself then that when I was grown, I was gonna have me not one, but two Cadillacs sitting out front of mama's and daddy's house. Well, sir, I guess you can say I've done a little better than that." Elvis bought his first Cadillac in March 1955 and purchased a pink Cadillac for his mother four months later. By 1957, he owned eight cars, four of them Cadillacs.

Poor Boy

- "When you look at things from the bottom up, they seem more wonderful than they really are."

Song Selection

- "I choose my own songs . . . I don't think there is anybody who can decide what I can do best, better than me. I think it would be a bad mistake if I had someone else telling me what to record, and how to record it, because I work strictly on instinct, impulse. I don't read music. My tastes might be a little different because I choose songs with the public in mind, and I try to, try to visualise it as though I am buying the record myself."

For the People

- "I hope I can continue to record good songs . . . that the people want to hear . . . the minute I stop pleasing them, I'm dead."

Several Million Fans Can't Be Wrong

- "I never thought I had a good voice . . . I just enjoy what I'm doing . . . and I put my heart and soul and body into it. I guess one of the reasons that people have liked it is because it was a little something different."

Screen Test

- Of his screen test with Hal Wallis of Paramount Pictures, Elvis said, "It's a dream come true. It's something I thought would never happen to me . . . of all people." Afterward, when asked if the studio executive told him he was good, he humbly responded, "No. They didn't say they thought I was good, they just told me that my test turned out real well." Six days after the test, on April 6, 1956, Elvis signed a seven year, three movie contract with Paramount.

Who Had the Last Laugh?

- "I thought people would laugh at me. Some did, and some are still laughing today, I guess."

The Man Behind the Man

- A combination of carnival sideshow promoter and slick salesman, Colonel Tom Parker knew how to turn Elvis into a money-making machine. About his signing with Parker for management, Elvis explained to Paul Wilder, "I was making quite a bit of money, but I wasn't as nationally known as I am now. The Colonel has a lot of friends in the entertainment business. He has connections; he knows lots of people that are important wheels in the business . . . He is an amusing guy. He plans stuff that nobody [else would] even think of." Interviewer Robert Brown asked Elvis what type of things the Colonel advised him on. "Everything!" Elvis quickly interjected. "He's the one guy that really gave me the big break . . . I don't know for sure where I would be if it weren't for him. Because he – he's a very smart man." Elvis often joked to friends, "We're the perfect combination: Colonel's an old carny, and me, I'm off the wall."

Don't Believe What You Read

- "I thought it was supposed to get easier, but it's getting worse. I hate having to read what people wrote 'bout me. I just hate it."

Just Another Headline

- On June 5, 1956, Elvis appeared on *The Milton Berle Show* and performed 'Hound Dog' with all the bumps and grinds he had become famous for. The next day, newspapers across the country carried stories about Elvis' "obscene performance". *Daily News* critic Ben Gross wrote that popular music "has reached its lowest depths in the 'grunt and groin' antics of one Elvis Presley." A few days later, *Journal American* writer Jack O'Brian described the performance as: "a display of primitive physical movement difficult to describe in terms suitable to a family newspaper." The reviews obviously annoyed Elvis some, because three weeks later he told reporter Charlotte Tuesday, "This Crosby guy [the critic for the *New York Herald-Tribune*], whoever he is, he says I'm obscene on the Berle show. Nasty. What does he know? . . . It's because I make more money . . . Them critics don't like to see nobody win doing any kind of music they don't know nothin' about . . . I don't care what they say, it ain't nasty." During the interview, Elvis nibbled on Tuesday's fingers, purportedly to get her attention. He did. When her story broke, the headline read: "Girl Reporter Bitten by Elvis" and another scandal broke.

Moving Target
- "A lot of these guys aren't reporters, they're marksmen."

Dreams Come True
- Elvis loved watching movies – a passion that continued throughout his life – and dreamed of becoming an actor. While in New York to record the TV soundtrack recordings for CBS's *Stage Show*, interviewer Robert Brown commented that Elvis used to go to a lot of movies. "Still do," he responded. "Every time we are in a place where I've got the time I usually go to a movie." A month later, Charlie Walker asked about Elvis signing his first movie contract. He explained it was "about the biggest thing" to have happened to his career thus far. "It's a dream come true, you know. Something I never [thought] would happen to me, of all people. But, it just shows you that you never can tell what's going to happen to you in life."

Gut Reaction
- "Trust your gut – it doesn't know how to lie."

Hollyweird

- Colonel Parker kept his promise to get Elvis into the movies, though they were not the serious acting roles Elvis had hoped for. Instead, he was thrust into formulated films, designed to generate money. "That's how it works. You get a record and you get on television and they take you to Hollywood to make a picture. But I wasn't ready for that town and they weren't ready for me . . . I did four pictures, so I got real good and used to the movie-star bit. Man, I'm sitting in the back of a Cadillac with sunglasses on and my feet propped up saying, 'I'm a movie star . . .' You know, eating hamburgers and drinking Pepsis and . . . totally nuts . . . I was living it up, man."

The Name on the Door

- "Hi, this is Elvis Presley. I'm just sitting here in my real fancy dressing room at 20th Century Fox, just before we start shooting *The Reno Brothers,* and I'd just like to tell everybody how good it makes me feel to see my name on the door of my own private dressing room and everything."

Don't Mess With Success

- "I had a letter recently suggesting that I should get drunk or something in my movies, but the type I'm making now are doing so well that it would be silly to change the formula. I've done 10 films and they've all made money. A certain type of audience likes me and it would be foolish to tamper with that kind of success."

Thumbs Down

- "Only thing worse than watchin' a bad movie is bein' in one."

Money Can't Buy Happiness

- Elvis was already a successful recording artist and movie star when in 1957, he confessed to Reverend Hamill, pastor of an Assembly of God congregation in Memphis, "I am the most miserable young man you have ever seen. I have got more money than I can ever spend, I have thousands of fans out there, and I have a lot of people who call themselves my friends, but I am miserable."

A Mess of Blues

- By the mid-sixties, Elvis had become increasingly discouraged at the way his career was progressing. He was particularly disgruntled with the acting roles the Colonel arranged in poorly scripted movies. During a drive from Hollywood to Memphis, Larry Geller claims Elvis confided to him: "How can I go back to making those teeny bopper movies after what I just went through? . . . I've got to go back and do things that have no meaning and are no help to humanity? Maybe I should just become a monk." The following year he recorded the gospel album, *How Great Thou Art*.

I've Got Rhythm

- "Rhythm is something you either have or you don't have, but when you have it, you have it all over."

In With the Mob

- Unlike some superstars today, Elvis loved his adoring fans and did not seem to mind them chasing after him. He told an interviewer with the *Oakland Tribune*, "If the police and my managers would let me, I'd get mobbed all the time. It makes you feel good. I would feel worse if they didn't swoon over me."

Car Collection

- "I suppose you know I've got a lot of cars. People have written about it in the papers and [they] write and ask me 'why?' When I was driving a truck, every time a big shiny car drove by, it started me sort of day dreamin'. I always felt that someday, somehow, something would happen to change everything for me and I'd daydream about how it would be. The first car I ever bought was the most beautiful car I've ever seen. It was second hand, but I parked it outside of my hotel the day I got it. I sat up all night just lookin' at it. And the next day the thing caught fire and burned up on the road." By early 1957, Elvis owned eight cars, "four of them [are] Cadillacs, one of them is a Lincoln Continental, and three little sports cars."

We're Comin' in Loaded

- "You know, when some people get down and out, they go out and get drunk and forget it all. Me, I just go out and buy another car. I've got money and I could buy anything there is to buy, but I still can't get out and mix with people like I'd like to do."

Fame and Fortune

- "Money can't buy what I want."

Excellence through Effort

- As driven as he was to improve upon his many talents, Elvis understood that expertise does not always come easily. "I like to progress . . . but I realise that it takes time. You can't bite off more than you can chew . . ."

Elvis on Elvis

- "I never expected to be anybody important. Maybe I'm not now, but whatever I am, whatever I will become, will be what God has chosen for me. Some people I know can't figure out how Elvis Presley happened. I don't blame them for wondering that. Sometimes I wonder myself . . . But no matter what I do, I don't forget about God. I feel he's watching every move I make. And in a way it's good for me. I'll never feel comfortable taking a strong drink, and I'll never feel easy smoking a cigarette. I just don't think those things are right for me . . . I just want to let a few people know that the way I live is by doing what I think God wants me to. I want someone to understand."

When to Stop

- "Just know where to draw the line."

Home Sweet Home

- "I'm going to keep Graceland as long as I possibly can," Elvis said, shortly after his release from the Army. Whenever he went off to record, tour, or to Hollywood to make movies, he always returned to Graceland to recharge. There he was surrounded, and isolated, with family and friends. "I only really feel at home in Memphis, at my own Graceland Mansion," he said. "A man gets lonesome for the things that are familiar to him – my friends and acquaintances." Home at Graceland was a 23 room mansion on 14 lush acres. There was a recording studio, the famous jungle room, a meditation garden, racquetball court, slot-car racetrack, rolling lawns for touch football games and golf carts to race around the grounds on. In August 1962, he told interviewer Lloyd Shearer, "I bought 10 acres right across the street from Graceland not too long ago," so he could expand the fun.

Giving it All Up

- "If I had to drop it all, I could do it, but I wouldn't like it."

The Eye of the Beholder

- Often asked to name who he thought was "the greatest country and western singer alive today," Elvis responded that he appreciated talent in all genres. "I like anybody that is good, regardless of what kind of a singer they are; whether they are religious, rhythm and blues, hillbilly, or anything else. If they're great, I like 'em . . . I just admire them if they are really great . . ."

Riding the Rainbow

- "Sometimes my teeth get tired of smiling. It's doggone tiring, but it's worth it. After all, you can't knock success."

Shake, Rattle and Roll

- One thing that drove female fans, in particular, wild about Elvis was his unique stage manner. It was those same movements that drove critics and parents crazy and caused some to want him stopped. "Man, I was tame compared to what they do now. Are you kidding? I didn't do anything but just jiggle," Elvis stated during a press conference prior to his record-breaking shows at New York's Madison Square Garden in 1972. From the onset of his career, he was criticised for his movements on stage. While performing in Jacksonville, Florida in 1956, he was called into Judge Marion Gooding's chambers and given orders to tone down his act. He told reporters, "I can't figure out what I'm doing wrong. I know my mother approves of what I'm doing." He did modify that show, replacing some of his movements with a wiggle of his pinky finger at the crowd – which drove them crazy – "I wiggled my finger and the girls went wild. I never heard screams like that in my life." On another occasion, he told a reporter, Ma'am, I'm not tryin' to be sexy. I didn't have any clear idea of trying to sell sex. It's just my way of expressin' how

I feel when I move around. It's all leg movement – I don't do nothin' with my body." To another, he explained, "Some people tap their feet, some people snap their fingers, and some people sway back and forth. I just sorta do 'em all together, I guess."

Staying Power
- When asked if he were a fad, Elvis responded, "You tell me – I wish I knew . . ."

Right Time, Right Place
- "I came along at a time in the music business when there was no trend. The people were looking for something different and I just came along in time."

A Classic
- "Somethin' can be real interestin' or different when it starts out, but if it can't change it's gonna die like Hula Hoops, or slow down a lot, like Silly Putty."

The Comeback Kid
- It started out as a Christmas special – that was Colonel Parker's idea – but Elvis refused to sing a Christmas song. He and executive producer Bob Finkle had a different vision, and in the end, they prevailed. Elvis sang some of his old hits in the round, just he and his original band. He was terrified. He had not performed before a live audience in years and was afraid the magic might be gone. But it all came back. For the closing number, he appeared alone in a white suit, standing before red lights that spelled out "E-L-V-I-S." He belted out the dramatic number 'If I Can Dream' and everyone knew – Elvis was back. Of the taping, he told a reporter, "I want you to know that I was scared to death, sir, when I did my first number for the

studio audience. Let me tell you, my knees were shaking, and it wasn't just from keeping time with the music. It's been so long since I worked before a live audience. But then it all came back to me, and it was just like doing a one-night stand in the old days." NBC broadcast the special on December 3, 1968. It was the highest rated program that week.

If They Could See Us Now

- "Only the other day, daddy looked at me and said, 'What happened, El? The last thing I remember is that I was working in a little ol' paint factory and you were driving a truck.'"

Elvis Has Left the Building

- "Wise men know when it's time to go."

WORK

Hard Work

- Elvis possessed a strong work ethic that was apparent from a young age. During his senior year of high school he was the primary support of his family. "I've never been accustomed to things real easy. I know it looks like I came up overnight. Not so! I can tell you that it was a lot of hard work. I've done plenty of it. I worked as a common labourer. I drove a truck for Crown Electrics in Memphis at the same time I was going to high school. I'd get up at 3.30 and be on the job at 6.30 for $12.50 a week. Luckily I don't need much sleep. I've got plenty of nervous energy." Eventually, the strain of school, work and no sleep caught up with him. He frequently fell asleep during class and was receiving failing marks. In time, his mother made Elvis quit his job and she went to work instead.

Have You Had Your V8?

- "Ambition is a dream with a V8 engine."

Still Standing

- "If they knock [you] down, get right back up. That's the only way to do it." When 17-year-old Vernon Elvis Presley eloped with 21-year-old Gladys Love Smith in June 1933, the young couple's prospects for future success were minimal. The working-class poor of the American rural South had always struggled, but with the nation locked in the grip of the Great Depression, conditions in the rough-and-tumble village of East Tupelo, Mississippi were particularly grinding. The newly-weds moved in with Vernon's parents, and he took out a $180 loan to build a two-room shotgun shack next door. When the couple moved in, just before Christmas 1934, there was no electricity or indoor plumbing.

Self Taught

- For his eleventh birthday, Elvis received a guitar from his parents and taught himself to play. "I took the guitar, and I watched people," Elvis recalled, "and I learned to play a little bit. But I would never sing in public. I was very shy about it, you know." As he grew older, he was rarely seen without his guitar in hand or slung over his back. During high school, he stored it in his locker until lunchtime. Then he would find a place to sit, sing to himself and strum, while he dreamed of appearing on the Grand Ole Opry.

Church Choir

- "No one in the family is in music," Elvis told a German reporter in 1959. "I guess I just love music so much, I decided to try and make a career out of it." From the age of two, Elvis evidenced an attraction to music. In the late 1930s, the family attended an Assembly of God church in East Tupelo, where Gladys's uncle was the preacher. Elvis escaped his mother's lap and scrambled up near the choir. He did not know the words they sang, but he could carry a tune. "I started singing [when] I was about three or four. I would sing in Church choir. Actually, what I was doing was yelling . . . some people still think that's what I do."

Vocal Styling

- "When I sang hymns back home with Mom and Pop, I stood still and looked like you feel when you sang a hymn. When I sing this rock'n'roll, my eyes won't stay open and my legs won't stand still. I don't care what they say, it ain't nasty."

It's a Sin

- "I have not sold my soul to the devil. It's only music!"

Voice Lessons

- A vocal coach might have squelched Elvis' unique vocal styling. Asked if he ever considered voice lessons he responded, "Not me. I'm not taking any chances. They just might train that thing – whatever it is – right out of my voice."

Rewired on Faith

- Elvis had faith in his talent and was willing to work hard to make it in the music business. Shortly after the release of Elvis' first recording, 'That's All Right, Mama', he quit his job driving a truck for Crown Electric and abandoned the idea of becoming an electrician. Then he devoted himself to launching his music career. Vernon was less confident about his son's potential. "My daddy had seen a lot of people who played guitars and stuff and didn't work, so he said: 'You should make up your mind, either about being an electrician or playing a guitar. I never saw a guitar player that was worth a damn.' Years later, he joked to a Las Vegas audience, "I was just out of high school and I was studying to be an electrician, and I got wired the wrong way!"

Just Like a Rolling Stone
- "I don't like to stay in one place very long."

Living in the Fast Lane
- "It's very seldom that I have an opportunity to talk to anybody, really, because the kind of life I lead; it moves very fast . . . You don't have much time to sit around."

On The Road Again
- In the early days of Elvis' career, he and his band worked three or four shows a day, six days a week. Then they drove through the night in a car – not a luxuriously out-fitted bus like touring artists today – to the next gig. Nevertheless, Elvis was doing what he wanted and he enjoyed it. "It was always exciting," he said. "We'd sleep in the back of the car, and we'd do a show and get offstage and get in the car and drive to the next town, and some-times just get there in time to wash up [and] do the show." The encouragement of fans, friends and disc jockeys infused him with energy and inspiration. He was grateful for their support and often expressed his gratitude. In an interview with Mae Axton, he said: "I'd like to personally thank you for really promoting my records down here,

because you really have done a wonderful job. And I really do appreciate it, because if you don't have people backing you – people pushing you – well, you might as well quit."

It's a Tough Business, but Someone Has to Do it

• Interviewer Ed Ripley asked Elvis if he liked the girls going wild over him, to which he quickly responded: "That's what keeps me in business."

Can You Sign this for Me?

• From the onset of Elvis' career, he cared about his fans and willingly signed every autograph possible: "I just wish there was some way to go round to every one of 'em and really show that you appreciate their liking you and all." Another time he explained, "lots of times them are crying . . . two or three hundred of them, crying around the stage door, and you'll have to sign a few autographs and close the door and leave, because the people want to close up the auditorium. It makes me feel real bad because I can't get to all of them." Four years later, when asked if it was annoying having fans hound him for autographs, he quickly responded, "No, it is not . . . if nobody came up and asked for an autograph . . . then you start to worry. As long as they come 'round . . . well, you know they still like you and it makes you feel good." Elvis never forgot that, without his fans, he wouldn't have a career. "After all, they are the people, mostly, that buy your records. They are the ones that go and ask their daddy for money to buy records . . . all I know is that wherever I go, I meet 'em by the hundreds, and they are just as nice as they can be."

A Very Lucky Human Being

• "I like the business I'm in. I like to entertain people," Elvis told Lloyd Shearer during the filming of *It Happened At The World's Fair*. "The money, or the financial end of it, is not the greatest aspect as far as I'm concerned. It can't be. Because if it was, it would show, and I wouldn't care about the other people; I wouldn't care about a performance that I gave . . . That's why I pick all my records and I try to pick the best songs possible. I try to do the best I can in the movies, you know, with the experience that I've gotten and everything. I think of myself strictly as a human being, who's, like I said, been very lucky."

Give them What they Want

- From the beginning of his career, Elvis possessed an inborn ability to read what his audience wanted, and he was only too happy to deliver it. "If I do something good, they let me know it. If I don't, they let me know that, too. It's a give-and-take proposition in that they give me back the inspiration. I work absolutely to them . . . They bring it out of me: the inspiration; the ham."

I Can't Sing, Dance or Play the Guitar

- A reviewer criticised both Elvis and his audience, calling them "idiots". The following day, on August 6, 1956, Elvis gave a lengthy interview to Paul Wilder at Lakeland, Florida's Polk Theater. Wilder seemed intent on stirring up further controversy, often trying to put Elvis on the defence. The reviewer had written that Elvis could not sing, dance or play the guitar. Wilder asked Elvis, "Can you play the guitar?" Without playing into Wilder's game, he responded without hesitation, "No. And I can't sing either, but somebody likes it." Wilder pressed further about his dancing. "No, [I] can't dance. I can't do nothin'."

Good Rockin'

- "Hi, this is Elvis Presley. I guess the first thing people want to know is 'Why I can't stand still when I'm singing?' Some people tap their feet, some people snap their fingers, and some people just sway back and forth. I just sort of do them all together, I guess. Singing rhythm and blues really knocks it out. I watch my audience and listen to 'em," Elvis shared in his 1956 taping for *The Truth About Me*. "I know that we're all getting something out of our system and none of us knows what that is. The important thing is . . . nobody's getting hurt."

The Good with the Bad

- Pressed about his reaction to some bad publicity he had generated, Elvis remained philosophical, telling interviewer Hy Gardner in a 1956 phone interview, "Well, sir, I tell you: you got to accept the bad along with the good. I've been getting some very good publicity – the press has been real wonderful to me – and I've been getting some bad publicity, but you have to expect that. I know that I'm doing the best that I can, and I have never turned a reporter down, and I've never turned a disc jockey down, because they're the people that help make you in this business . . . As long as I know that I'm doing the best I can."

Separation of Church and Stage

- After using the derogatory term "holy roller" to reference members of the Assembly of God church Elvis attended, a reporter tried to make a connection between Elvis' stage moves and his perceived religious worship service: "There was some article that came out where I got the jumpin' around from my religion. My religion has nothing to do with what I do now," Elvis responded firmly, "because the type of stuff I do now is not religious music. My background had nothing to do with the way I sing."

Got My Mojo Working

- When Elvis played Ottawa, Canada in April 1957, interviewer Mac Lipson informed Elvis that a local school board had made a motion to encourage students and teachers to stay away from Elvis' shows because they considered his singing – or more specifically, his stage movements – vulgar. "I certainly don't mean to be vulgar," he told Lipson, "and I don't think I am . . . That's just my way of expressing songs. You have to put on a show for the people." That he gave the audience an entertaining show, worthy of their time and money spent, was of the utmost importance to Elvis: "You can't stand there like a statue."

It's a Clean Show

- "I wouldn't do anything vulgar in front of anybody . . . My folks didn't bring me up that way. I just move with the music. It's the way I feel."

You've Got Mail

- For the first two years of Elvis' career he was receiving 30–60 letters from fans each week. He enjoyed reading their comments about his songs and performance, and answered each of them personally, including a photograph with each response. By 1956, the amount of fan mail he received was staggering and he was forced to employ nine secretaries to do "nothing but answer mail". By August of that year, he said, "they're about 25,000 letters behind" in answering his mail. It concerned him so much that he taped a message to his fans stating: "If you don't get your card or letter answered [right away], don't think they were just ignoring you, because you will hear from us. It may take a little time, but just as quick as they can get caught up, we will. I'll make darn sure that you get an answer, because we certainly appreciate all the thousands of letters that are coming every day. At least we've given the postman in Nashville something to do. Well, I guess that's about all we've got to say, so you keep writing in, and don't feel bad if you don't get an answer right away, because we'll answer you as quick as we can. Bye, bye."

Song Search

- Speaking of his choice of songs, Elvis told a reporter, "I've gone through more than 100 numbers to get just one that I thought was right."

Elvis at Work

- "The RCA Victor people can tell you that when I cut my records and there's no audience to watch me, I still sing the same way: with my whole body. It's just my way of putting everything I have into a song. A doctor once told me I used up more energy in a few minutes of singing then lots of men use up in a whole working day."

For the Record

- Elvis was passionate about getting the best performance on tape for his records. It was normal for him to work until early hours of the morning, recording take after take, until he felt it was right. It was important to him that he give his fans his best. "Long after I'm gone, what I did today will be heard by someone. I just want them to get the best of what I had."

I'm a Believer

- "I don't attend church regular," Elvis shared in 1956 – at the time, he was playing six to seven shows a week, two-to-four shows a day, which regularly included a

Sunday matinee – "but I'm a true believer in God. I believe that all good things come from God."

Fulfilling Obligations

- Elvis received his draft notice in December 1957. Production on his next film, *King Creole*, had been postponed until January. Concerned about the time and resources already invested in the production, Elvis wanted to complete the picture before reporting for duty. He wrote to the Memphis Draft board requesting a deferment, "so these folks will not lose so much money, with all they have done so far."

Soldier Boy

- It is difficult to imagine Elvis being concerned that his popularity might diminish while he served in the army, but days before he was inducted a reporter asked him that very thing. Elvis responded saying, "That's the sixty-four-dollar question. I wish I knew." Years later, he commented, "I got drafted, shafted and everything else. So overnight it was all gone. It was like it never happened, like a dream . . ."

You're in the Army Now

- As word spread that the Memphis Draft Board would soon issue Elvis' draft notice, every major branch of the military vied for his service. The air force wanted him to tour recruitment centres, the navy wanted to create the Elvis Presley Company, but he refused their offers. "It's a duty I've got to fill, and I'm gonna do it," he said. "I guess the only thing I'll hate about it is leaving my mama. She's always been my best girl." It was important to him that he fulfil his obligation with no special treatment, as a regular soldier would. "My induction notice says for me to leave my car at home, as transportation will be provided. They tell me just to bring a razor, a toothbrush, a comb and enough money to last two weeks."

Reporting for Duty

- "I'm going into the service and do the best I can. If they want me to sing for the boys, I'll sing. If they want me to march – anything they want me to do is all right."

Pieces of My Life

- Returning to the States, and his career, Elvis reflected on his military service to a reporter: "People were expecting me to mess up; to goof up in one way or another. They thought I couldn't take it and so forth. I was determined to go to any limits to prove otherwise. Not only to the people who were wondering, but to myself too." Then he set about proving he was still the King of rock'n'roll.

Lonely Man

- Although Elvis loved hard work and entertaining, he was often lonely and once confided, "A lot of times I feel miserable; don't know which-a-way to turn."

In the Blood

- In his first extended telephone interview from Germany, while serving in the army, Elvis told Memphis DJ Keith Sherriff he couldn't imagine a career outside of show business. "That's probably it, one way or another, whether it's singing or working as a stagehand. You know, once it gets in your blood, it's hard to stay away from it."

Previously Unreleased Thank You

- While still serving in the army, stationed in Germany, Elvis wants to record a message to his fans, expressing his sincere gratitude for their support. In January 1959, he wrote the Colonel requesting RCA make arrangements for him to do so: "I want to be able to thank them, not only for buying my records and for their loyalty to me, but also for the help they have given me in deciding the kind of songs to sing . . . I'm deeply grateful to them, and I want them to know it. When I'm out of the army recording again, I will always listen to their ideas, just as I did before. I just wanted to let my fans know how I feel. Sincerely, Elvis." The request was never honoured.

Returning to the Limelight

- As Elvis neared the end of his army service, he was asked if he were anxious about returning to his music and acting career. "Yes, I am," he answered. "I have my doubts . . . The only thing I can say, is that I'm gonna try. I'll be in there fighting."

Scratch and Fight

- A couple months after his thirtieth birthday, Elvis reflected on how far he had come from his impoverished Tupelo, Mississippi beginnings to his current wealth and success. "I can never forget longing to be someone," he told *Memphis Commercial Appeal* writer James Kingsley, "I guess if you are poor you always think bigger and want more than those who have everything . . . I know what it is to scratch and fight for what you want."

A Job Well Done

- "Happiness is knowin' you've done a good job, whether it's professional or for another person."

Anything Worth Doing . . .

- "Take the time to do a thing right. Otherwise, why do it?"

Film Work

- "I'm trying to make it in acting, you know. And it takes a long time, a lot of work, and a lot of experience. But I'm trying to make it that way. And if I can get established that way, I'm okay."

Keep Trying

- "In the entertainment business, the future is very uncertain . . . So I'm only going to say, 'I'll try to continue to please the people enough that they keep liking me, and keep interested.' . . . As far as knowing what the future holds for me, I've got no idea."

All Work and No Play . . .

- "I like to work. I like to have a little time off, too, where I don't have to do anything – which I've had very little of since I've been out of the army . . ."

It's a Tough Job

- "I really get tired of being Elvis."

Elvis the Shepherd

- The Colonel kept Elvis on a gruelling work schedule. Early in his career, it was not uncommon for him to work six and seven days a week. He routinely got only four or five hours of sleep a night. Asked why he didn't slow down a little, he explained, "the Lord can give and . . . the Lord can take away. I might be herding sheep next year."

All Shook Up

- "I don't calm down 'till two or three hours after I leave the stage. Sometimes I think my heart is going to explode."

European Fans

- For years Elvis talked about touring Europe, particularly

after being stationed in Germany. In the early 1970s, Elvis taped a message directed towards his European fans: "I really love their devotion and we've got to come see 'em – we've got to. I've been saying for years, but we love 'em." The promised tour never materialised. Many speculated that Colonel Parker was an illegal alien and feared he would be caught and deported if he left the United States, and that he did not want his mega-star client touring abroad without him.

Goals

- Several days before his screen-test, Elvis shared, "I would like to learn how to act in the movies, I really would . . . I think if you really try and set your head to it, you can probably do it."

Memorisation

- Never having "read a line . . . studied acting or been in any plays," Elvis did not know how to prepare for his first movie role, so he memorised not just his own lines, but the entire *Love Me Tender* script. "I have no trouble memorising. I once memorised General MacArthur's farewell address, and I can still reel off Lincoln's Gettysburg speech from when I memorised it in school."

Acting Class

- Over the years, Elvis had watched hundreds of movies, taking in the performances of the best and worst actors of the day. It was his acting school, of sorts. "I learned a lot from studying the movies I've been to . . . watching to find out how it's done." As he made the move into acting, he was often asked if he were planning to study the craft. "I don't think you learn to become an actor," he said. "I think you just – maybe you've got a bit of acting talent and

81

you develop it . . . If you learn to be an actor, in other words, if you're not a real actor – you're false." In the beginning, he was compared to Marlon Brando and James Dean, whom he called "a genius at acting." In a 1956 interview with Lloyd Shearer, Elvis said, "I've made a study of Marlon Brando. I've made a study of poor Jimmy Dean. I've made a study of myself, and I know why girls, at least the young 'uns, go for us. We're sullen, we're broodin', we're something of a menace. I don't understand it exactly, but that's what the girls like in men. I don't know anything about Hollywood, but I know you can't be sexy if you smile. You can't be a rebel with a grin."

Acting Ambition

- Although Elvis made over 30 feature films, he was never able to realise his dream of becoming a serious dramatic actor. On the set of *The Trouble With Girls*, Elvis confided to co-star Marilyn Mason that, "I'd like to make one good film before I leave. I know this town's laughing at me." In an interview for the documentary *Elvis On Tour*, Elvis said of his films: "It was a job. That's how I treated it. But I cared so much I became physically ill. I didn't have final approval on the script, which means that I couldn't tell you 'This is good for me.' I don't think anyone was consciously trying to harm me. It was just Hollywood's image of me was wrong and I knew it, and I couldn't say anything about it, couldn't do anything about it. I was never indifferent. I was so concerned until that's all I talked about . . . I had thought they would . . . give me a chance to show some kind of acting ability or do a very interesting story, but it did not change. It did not change, and so I became very discouraged . . ."

Bankable Schlock

- "It was getting harder and harder singing to the camera all day long. Let's face it, when you have 10 different songs for each movie, they can't all be good. Eventually, I got tired of singing to turtles and guys I'd just beaten up."

I Feel So Bad

- "When I don't do a good job, I know it and I'm blue as hell. You'll pardon my language, but I mean it."

TCB to TLC

- "Takin' Care of Business" was an Elvis anthem: "The best thing you can do is get in there, no horsin' around, and take care of business," he said. Elvis and Priscilla sketched a lightning bolt with "TCB" over it and had a jeweller craft a medallion as a thank-you gift – and to make amends for his bad temper – for the members of his Las Vegas stage show and entourage. The gifts were so well received that he had more made up to give to his celebrity friends. He later had a female version made with "TLC" for "Tender Lovin' Care", another Elvis credo.

Rip it Up

- "If a cause is just, you fight for it . . . you gouge out their . . . eyes."

Money Making Machine

- Despite the fact that Elvis and Colonel Parker sometimes disagreed about career choices, particularly the ridiculously scripted movies Parker placed his client in, there was a bond between them – and together they became incredibly wealthy. In a 1960's conversation, Elvis told the Colonel, "You've been good to me. You put a lump in my throat." To which Parker replied, "Thank you son. You put a lump in my wallet."

Compromise Has its Benefits

- "Make your money doin' it their way – if you have to – then do what you want."

CPAs

- "I have no need for bodyguards, but I have very specific uses for two highly trained certified public accountants."

Working Class

- Elvis was a multi-millionaire who could buy anything he wanted – and did. Not only for himself, but for his family, entourage, and even strangers. With all his wealth, he remained humble and gracious. It was not the rich, but the working class – those whose backgrounds were most similar to his own – that he related to. "They're the people with values I understand," he said.

The Business of Elvis

- "I can't get into my head that I'm property. People tell me you can't do this or that, but I don't listen to them. I do what I want. I can't change, and I won't change."

If it Ain't Broke

- It is easy to look at someone else's life and tell them what opportunities they should take advantage of or choices they should make. Elvis received his share of advice about what songs he should record, pictures he should make, clothes he should wear on and offstage, who he should or should not date, and much more. "I'd like to progress, but I realise that you can't bite off more than you can chew; you have to know your capabilities. I have people say to me all the time, 'Why don't you do an artistic picture? Why don't you do this picture [or] that picture?' . . . Well, I would like to, I would like to do something someday where I feel that I have really done a good job . . . But I feel that it will come with time and a little living . . . I think that it will come eventually, you know, that's my goal . . . In the meantime, if I can entertain people with the things that I am doing, I would be a fool to tamper with it or try to change it . . . You don't get many chances in this business, that's the sad part about it. So you are better off – if what you are doing is doing okay – you're better off sticking with it 'till just time itself changes things. I mean, that's the way I believe, really."

James Bond

- "I've had people ask me if I was going to sing in the movies, and I'm not, as far as I know." That's what Elvis thought – but Colonel Parker had other ideas. Elvis wanted to be a serious actor, and did not think it made sense to put a song into a film simply to have him sing it. The Colonel thought that fans would spend more money on the films if Elvis sang. So he did. "I wasn't exactly James Bond in the movies," Elvis said, "but then, no one asked Sean Connery to sing while dodging bullets."

Self Criticism

- Shortly after the July 1957 release of Elvis' first film, *Loving Me Tender*, Vancouver DJ Red Robinson asked Elvis to rate himself as an actor. "Pretty bad," he said. "I mean, that's something you can learn through experience. I think that maybe I might accomplish something at it through the years." Elvis went on to do another 30 films.

Times Have Changed

- In the latter part of Elvis' career, he was asked what he thought of the wild antics and stage performances of rock' n'roll artists of the 1960s. "Man, I was tame compared to what they do now . . . I didn't do anything but just jiggle."

Biography

1935–1945

Elvis Aron Presley was born January 8, 1935, 35 minutes after stillborn elder brother Jesse Garon. It had been a difficult pregnancy, and the Presleys were never to have another child. Right from the beginning, family members recalled Gladys as being an anxious and protective mother, and consistently described her relationship with her surviving son as being unusually close. Vernon continued to work odd jobs when he could find them, but his near-total lack of ambition was not conducive to securing long-term employment. His role in a $4 cheque altering scheme earned Vernon a three-year sentence to Parchman Prison. The sentence was suspended after eight months, and Vernon was released in February 1939, but by then the Presleys had lost their tiny home. What followed was a series of cheap rented rooms and stays with various family members as Vernon drifted from job to job, continuing until Elvis was old enough to begin school.

It was during these early years that the most influential relationship of Elvis' life was forged. Much has been made of the connection that existed between Elvis and his mother. "Unusually close" are the words that biographers and family members most typically use to describe it, always with the unspoken implication that observers generally recognised something peculiar about the relationship, but were never able to identify exactly what it was. In the absence of an obvious explanation, speculation has sometimes run to the unsavoury, but there is no evidence to support that claim. More likely, the bond grew out of Gladys' need for emotional comfort and security that her ineffectual husband was unable to provide. Elvis simply adapted to his mother's needs, doing what many children do in similar situations: he developed the ability to sense what others wanted from him, and then mirrored that back. This ability was later demonstrated in Elvis' interaction with the press and with his fans.

To say that Elvis was merely a mama's boy is to gloss over the complexity of their bond. He was the centre of Gladys' life, to be sure, and probably excessively coddled and catered to. They spoke to one another in baby talk throughout their lives, calling each other by pet names.

The war years found the Presleys back in East Tupelo, with Elvis attending the local grade school and Vernon periodically drifting in and out of his family's life as he worked short-term construction jobs in the area. By August 1945 he had saved up $200 to put a down payment on a small home.

1945–1952

Elvis' first public performance came at the instigation of his fifth-grade teacher, who entered the shy 10-year-old in a radio-sponsored talent contest at the October 1945 Mississippi-Alabama Fair and Dairy Show. He reportedly stood on a chair in order to reach the microphone and, without accompaniment, sang 'Old Shep': a sad song about a boy and his dog. Years later, Elvis recalled that he won fifth place, and later got a whipping from his mother, probably for riding some of the more "dangerous" carnival rides.

The lack of musical accompaniment was somewhat rectified several months later on Elvis' eleventh birthday, with the gift of a guitar. He recalled wanting a bicycle instead, but was convinced by his mother that a guitar would help with his singing (not to mention being considerably less costly). Several relatives and neighbours taught the boy a few basic chords, but it was the youthful Pastor Frank Smith who provided the most consistent instruction.

That summer the Presleys moved into town, first to a rented shack across the road from the poor black section of Tupelo called Shake Rag, then to a more respectable "coloured" neighbourhood. Although the family certainly did not consider themselves as such, these living arrangements labelled them as poor white trash in the eyes of the white community. Remarkably, given the place and time, the Presleys seemed to be free of the prevailing racial prejudice directed against their neighbours. Elvis was particularly taken with the music, sartorial style, and religious expression that surrounded him. That, coupled with his fondness for what classmates termed "trashy hillbilly" and "race" music, singled Elvis out even further, making him more of an outsider. Several classmates later remembered him bringing his guitar to school and shyly strumming on it during recess, but few stopped to listen and even fewer were impressed.

Although some grade school contemporaries later claimed to have noted emerging signs of musical prodigy, these recollections were most likely manufactured in hindsight. Few of Elvis' classmates at the time seemed to even be aware of him, let alone consider that he had any particular ability. If they thought of him at all, it was as a sad, bashful, awkward loner who flew under the schoolyard radar. His teachers, later pressed for memories of their illustrious former student, recalled Elvis the same way they recalled the hundreds of other children who passed unremarkably through their classrooms: quiet, polite, average. Just the sort of vague recollection one is likely to have about an undistinguished student who attracted little notice at the time. Although never stated in so many words, the overall impression given is of a lonely and dreamy boy, quietly absorbing everything he sees and hears; assembling bit by bit the singular persona he will one day unleash on an astonished world. In other words, he was learning how to be Elvis Presley.

Predictably, it did not take long for Vernon to exhaust the few job opportunities that were open to him in Tupelo. The Presleys sold off their furniture, loaded their few belongings into the car and, once again, moved on. Elvis finished out his eighth grade year at Humes High School in Memphis, Tennessee largely unnoticed. Circumstances changed dramatically in 1949, when the family was accepted into Lauderdale Courts. For the Presleys, their two-bedroom, $35-a-month, government housing project apartment represented a level of comfort and luxury that had previously been unattainable. Gladys later remembered her family's stay at the Courts as being the happiest years of her life. Whatever Elvis may have thought of his new home, it was nearby Beale Street, with its businesses and clubs that catered to a primarily "coloured" clientele, which irresistibly drew his attention. The young boy was a frequent visitor, soaking in the sights and sounds, although yet too shy to venture beyond the sidewalk.

School work alternated with a brief stint as a drill press operator at Precision Tool Co., until it was discovered that Elvis was underage. Later jobs included movie theatre usher, upholstery supply clerk, and finally, metal furniture assembler, which lasted until the beginning of his senior year. By then, the exhausted Elvis fell asleep in class so frequently that his mother forced him to quit his after-school job, even though his weekly pay cheque was a significant contribution to the family's meagre finances. Elvis craved attention, especially the acceptance of his male peers, but that acceptance had always eluded him. The distinctive style he had recently developed had much to do with it. The greased-back hair, long sideburns, and flamboyant clothes that favoured pink and black colour combinations were little appreciated by the members of the high school football team that he had unsuccessfully attempted to join the previous year. The flashy clothing and obsessive combing of his hair proved to be a lightning rod for teasing and derogatory remarks; remarks Elvis outwardly took in a good-natured fashion, but which rankled him terribly within. Most of his classmates dismissed Elvis as weird – a gawky white boy who favoured negro clothing and negro music – but that was about to change.

1953

The programme of the Humes High School annual Minstrel Show that April listed the sixteenth act of the evening as "Guitarist – Elvis Prestly". His rendition of ''Til I Waltz With You', a song made popular by Teresa Brewer, came as a surprise to his classmates, almost none of whom knew that Elvis could sing. That evening marked a profound shift in the attitude of his peers. "It was amazing how popular I became after that," Elvis later recalled. In keeping with his unique style sense, he attended the Senior Prom that year wearing a pink tuxedo.

Following graduation, Elvis applied for a variety of sales clerk positions, but was turned down for each one on the basis of his appearance. "Rather flashily dressed 'playboy' type" is how the interview paperwork reads, although it also notes that he was a hard worker. Elvis ended up back at

Precision Tool Co. He was, by this time, providing the primary financial support of his family.

A pivotal moment in the history of modern music occurred that summer, although no one recognised it at the time. Perhaps if they had, there would be more details and fewer variations in the accounts of how Elvis Presley arrived at the Memphis Recording Service that summer. The simplest version has him wanting to make a recording as a present for his mother. The resulting two-sided acetate cost $3.98 and featured Elvis accompanying himself with his guitar on the sentimental tunes 'My Happiness' and 'That's When Your Heartaches Begin'.

1954

Elvis returned to the Memphis Recording Service studio in January, ostensibly to record two more songs, but probably in the hopes of being discovered. This time his singing style caught the attention of office manager Marion Keisker, who alerted owner Sam Phillips. Phillips also recognised something unique about the nervous young man's performance, but did not yet know what to do with it.

It was around this same time that Elvis began attending worship services at the First Assembly of God church in South Memphis, whose membership included the Blackwood Brothers, a leading gospel quartet. While his parents favoured the group's smooth harmonies, and the family faithfully attended their performances at the all-night gospel singing held at Ellis Auditorium, Elvis was consistently drawn to the more energetic style of another gospel group, the Statesmen. Elvis particularly admired the free-spirited leg shaking of bass singer Jim "Big Chief" Wetherington, and the soaring vocal style of lead singer Jake Hess. Both of these qualities would later be manifested in Elvis' own onstage performances.

White gospel was not the only music that sparked Elvis' interest. He would frequently sneak out during the sermon at the Assembly of God to catch the impassioned preaching and singing at the "coloured" church down the road, then hurry to get back before he was missed. Church was only one of the many places in Memphis where musical inspiration could be found. Weekend radio broadcasts brought country & western favourites and the occasional hillbilly tune from The Grand Old Opry in Nashville and the Louisiana Hayride in Shreveport. Closer to home was the blues and R&B and boogie that drifted out of Beale Street bars, mingling with the other sights and sounds that Elvis found so enticing there. He was a regular at Charlie's Record Shop, where he went to listen to – and buy, as frequently as his slim finances allowed – the negro blues and R&B recordings he so loved.

Finally tired of being razzed about his long hair, Elvis quit his job at Precision Tool and found work driving a delivery truck for an electrical company, with the intention of one day becoming a licensed electrician. A much hoped for audition with the Songfellows, a junior version of the Blackwood Brothers, ended in disappointment when Elvis was bluntly told that he couldn't sing. Various auditions followed in a variety of settings, but all yielded the same verdict: "You just can't sing." Whether fair or not, the reality was simply that Elvis did not sing like anybody else.

In July, Sam Phillips was working with a raucous country & western combo called the Starlight Wranglers who were in need of a singer. Elvis came to mind. The connection was not an obvious one, so it may be that Phillips empathised with a punk kid's hunger to succeed and wanted to give him a break. Phillips later recounted having seen an electric company delivery truck parked at the curb outside his recording studio many times during the previous months, and wondered if Elvis had been sitting out there trying to work up the nerve to come inside. At any rate, a meeting was arranged at the studio, which turned into an unexpected recording session, and the near-accidental result was 'That's All Right'. A few days later, Phillips passed a copy of the recording to a local radio DJ, who played it during his evening broadcast. The resulting audience response convinced Phillips that he was on to something. 'Blue Moon of Kentucky' was quickly recorded as a B-side. That Saturday night, Elvis performed the two songs at a local club, with the Starlight Wranglers backing him up. On Monday, Phillips drew up a recording contract, which the Presleys signed for their underage son, and the legend of Sun Records was born. Two weeks later, Elvis performed his two numbers on the bill of a Louisiana Hayride package show that was booked into town at the Overton Park Shell. His leg gyrations and raw vocalising reportedly drove the crowd wild that night, sparking sales that soon landed the single on *Billboard*'s regional country & western charts.

At this stage, Elvis was fronting a three-man group that also included former Starlight Wranglers Scotty Moore on guitar and Bill Black on stand-up bass. Their usual act featured cornball jokes and clownish antics that sometimes veered toward the vulgar, interspersed with three or four guitar-pounding, melody shredding songs. The highlight was when Bill jumped up on his bass and rode it like a bucking bronco as he continued to play. Throughout, Elvis pranced and wiggled and shook his leg as if infected with St Vitus dance. Although his was only a small opening act, even the big name entertainers hated having to follow Elvis.

He invariably stole the show, leaving audiences spent and drained of energy. It was an unlucky performer who had to follow him.

Phillips was able to secure his rising young star an appearance at the Grand Old Opry in October. It was a dream-come-true for Elvis, but one which both awed and terrified him. He bounded out to the microphone after being introduced and sang his one song, but the performance drew a lukewarm response. Adult audiences simply did not know what to make of Elvis Presley. A November appearance at the Louisiana Hayride was an unqualified success, however, yielding a one-year contract to perform on the popular Saturday night broadcasts. Once again, the Presleys signed the paperwork for their underage son.

The year finished out with the release of two more Sun singles and a series of short tours through the southern states. Elvis, Scotty and Bill drove in shifts from venue to venue, with their instruments strapped to the roof of the car. The obligation to return to Shreveport for their weekly Hayride broadcasts limited the audience the group could reach. Those who witnessed some of these earliest performances described their shock at first seeing Elvis onstage. He was a pimply, greasy-haired guy with mascara'd lashes and – could it be true? – blue eye shadow! His stage wardrobe at the time sometimes combined a red jacket with bright green trousers, worn with a pink shirt and socks, and two-tone shoes. The rawboned young singer had a look of questionable personal hygiene about him, and sometimes spat a wad of gum onto the stage just prior to singing. Yet in spite of that – or perhaps, because of it – teenage audiences screamed so loud that the musicians were often unable to hear their own instruments, let alone Elvis singing.

Not every teenager was enthralled – male audience

members were frequently less than impressed – but their dates regularly worked themselves into hysterics. Elvis may not have known what he was doing onstage at this point, but he was learning his craft at an accelerated rate. He took it all in, mentally noting what worked and what did not, utilising his lifelong ability to sense what people wanted from him and to reflect that back. The more the audiences screamed, the more Elvis gave them, and over the course of the next year he honed his onstage performance to perfection.

1955

1955 began much as 1954 had ended: short regional tours alternating with Louisiana Hayride broadcasts. The only difference was that the crowds were getting larger, the girls were screaming louder, and Elvis was increasingly becoming a lightning rod for critical attack. What is amazing is how well he managed to handle it all.

Today, when the mass media serves up pop icons by the ladleful on a daily basis – their images carefully polished and their responses coached by a slew of professional handlers – it is difficult to imagine that there was a time when none of that existed. Bandleaders had their followings, film stars had their fans; Sinatra had left bobbysoxers swooning in the aisles a few years previously, but there had never been anything approaching the pandemonium that Elvis produced. There was no one to coach him; no one to offer advice about how to handle the antagonistic press or the clothes-tearing fans. No one could tell Elvis what to do because no one had ever experienced – perhaps even imagined – anything like the phenomenon that Elvis Presley became. He was the first pop music icon; he originated the concept, and he was left to figure out how to do it on his own.

Part of what enabled Elvis to cope was his innate personal charm. His unfailing respectful politeness, coupled with sincere enthusiasm, melted the hearts of critics who liked him and disarmed those who did not. Even his most ardent detractors frequently found themselves unable to muster the same level of vitriol once they had interviewed him. Many of them eventually became fans.

Sometime early in the year, Elvis came to the attention of Colonel Tom Parker: an astute personal manager and show promoter with a genius for marketing and public relations. He was known for devoting all his energies to a single client at a time, and had built the careers of country music legends Eddy Arnold and Hank Snow, each in turn.

Parker was not a legitimate Colonel; that was merely an honorary title which he exploited to maximum benefit. In truth, there was little about Parker that was legitimate. He had a shadowy past that he kept secret by never letting anyone get too close. To his credit, Parker was a man of integrity in that, once a deal had been finalised, he was committed to honouring it. He was also coarse, tough, pushy, and abrasive; a bit of a con man who could feign affability when it suited his purposes, but who was at heart a cynical carny huckster. His one passion appeared to be for making business deals: he was a relentless negotiator who could talk anyone into anything; and if he could draw blood while doing it, so much the better. Parker lived for beating out a competitor, and always had his eye open for the next big opportunity. Dollar signs did not appear in his eyes the first time Parker saw Elvis perform – that came later – but he was interested enough to watch and wait. He did not have to wait long.

It is difficult to determine when it was that the first press writer realised that "Elvis" rhymed with "pelvis", but once the connection was made, the two words became inextricably linked. The description was accurate and the implication was sexually suggestive. The name stuck and, right or wrong, played a part in building Elvis' image.

When he playfully ended a performance in Jacksonville, Florida by saying, "Girls, I'll see you backstage," the crowd rushed the stage. Police arrived to find that hundreds of screaming fans had cornered Elvis in the locker room and torn off most of his clothing. It was this incident that convinced Colonel Parker of the young singer's potential. From that point on, Parker began to manoeuvre himself into sole control over Elvis' career.

The opportunity came near the end of the year. Sun Records was a regional operation, lacking the distribution capacity and clout to break its acts on a national level. Elvis' Sun releases had not gotten attention beyond the regional charts, and even then it was the country & western listings. Colonel Parker had bigger plans; he wanted Elvis out of the contract with Sun and more importantly, outside the influence of Sam Phillips. Phillips was canny enough to recognise the power play and set the price of a contract buyout at $35,000. That amount of money may seem ridiculous now, but $35,000 was an unheard of sum at the time, especially in view of the fact that the current contract was set to expire only a few months later anyway. But Parker did not want to wait; the time to cash in on Elvis' popularity was now.

Many expected that rock'n'roll would fail to last out the year. Certainly there were few who thought that it was anything more than just a passing craze. Parker hoped to buy in cheaply, make a killing, and get out with a hefty profit before the bubble burst. He convinced RCA Records to purchase the contract, as well as Sun's existing Elvis catalogue, and managed to cut himself in on the deal besides. The five Sun singles were re-released on the RCA label, but this time on the Pop charts. Press releases in *Cashbox* and *Billboard* magazines exploited the deal for all it was worth.

1956

The first RCA recording sessions, held in January, were a disaster. Elvis struggled to recapture the creative inspiration that Sam Phillips had extracted from him in the tiny Sun studio. He had connected with the way Phillips allowed a recording to evolve, and felt uncomfortable in the strange new surroundings. RCA executives became convinced that the signing had been a huge mistake and started looking around for someone to blame. Perhaps even Parker began to doubt. Finally, the session produced a cut that Elvis was pleased with. 'Heartbreak Hotel' was released at the end of the month, reaching number one on the national charts in April and selling over one million copies. Elvis had earned his first hit record.

National television exposure came close behind, with four appearances on a weekly show hosted by big bandleaders Tommy and Jimmy Dorsey. With the exception of a couple of dates in Ohio, these appearances marked the first time Elvis had performed outside the South, as well as being his television debut. The following month found him in Hollywood for a screen test. He performed two scenes from *The Rainmaker* and lip synched to 'Blue Suede Shoes'. Studio executives were unimpressed with the dramatic sequences, but agreed that the musical performance was electrifying.

Parker delivered these opportunities as a gesture of good faith, but withheld the actual contracts until his new client was firmly locked in. He had already been successful in winning over Elvis' parents by playing up his ability to protect their boy from harm. Elvis accepted the mobbing by fans and frequent vandalising of his cars by souvenir-hunters as the price of fame, but his mother viewed these events with terror. The image of Parker as a surrogate father figure was plainly incongruous, but Gladys' increasing fear for the safety of her only child was such that she was willing to believe anyone who told her what she wanted to hear. If Elvis had any misgivings about Parker, they were quickly brushed aside in his desire to allay his mother's concerns.

The resulting management agreement with Elvis gave Parker sole and exclusive rights to any and all public and private appearances. When the ink was dry, the Elvis Presley media blitz kicked into high gear. In quick succession, Parker bought out Elvis' recently renewed contract with Louisiana Hayride for $10,000, signed a seven-picture film deal with Hollywood producer Hal Wallis, and booked Elvis into a two-week gig in Las Vegas.

While the Vegas shows were rather unenthusiastically received at first, Elvis was having the time of his life. He had women, money, fancy cars and fame; what was there not to like? Things only got better in May, when his debut RCA album titled *Elvis Presley* reached the top of *Billboard*'s album charts. The record stayed at number one for 10 weeks, ending the year as the label's biggest seller to date.

Not everybody was as happy as Elvis was with the direction his life was taking him. The antagonism that his stage performances continued to generate can scarcely be imagined today. Accusations directed at him ranged from contributing to the delinquency of youth to inciting riot. He was regularly denounced from the pulpit and in the press. The most vehement protests came from those who saw in Elvis a racial threat against white America.

Perhaps the furore is best measured by a report given to

F.B.I. director J. Edgar Hoover, which stated that Elvis' act amounted to nothing more than "sexual self-gratification onstage". Given what has since been revealed about Hoover's secret sexual proclivities, that characterisation must have been terribly thrilling to him. Elvis' bump and grind version of 'Hound Dog' during a June guest appearance on the *Milton Berle Show* did not help matters. Reviews in the national press the following day expressed outrage, ranging from "Mr Presley has no discernable singing ability", to "[Pop music] has reached its lowest depths in the 'grunt and groin' antics of one Elvis Presley." Of course the louder the press decried Elvis' gyrations, the louder his fans screamed for more.

Finally, even Colonel Parker – a firm believer that any publicity was good publicity – began to wonder if his client had gone too far. Elvis continued to defend his behaviour in interviews: "I don't even smoke or drink . . . I started singing as a gospel singer and come from a Christian home." While he always maintained that his performance style was a reflection of innocent enthusiasm, rather than crass calculation, Elvis was clearly not oblivious to the effect his onstage movements produced. He was, however, mystified by the vehemence of the criticism levelled at him, and remained steadfast in the sincerity of his motives: "If I did think I was bad for people," Elvis declared, "I would go back to driving a truck, and I really mean this." Nevertheless, he did back off for a time.

It was a noticeably subdued Elvis who performed on the *Steve Allen Show* the following month. In a televised interview later that evening, talk-show host Hy Gardner asked Elvis if he had learned anything from his critics. "No, I haven't," Elvis responded politely, "I don't feel like I'm doing anything wrong."

The demure Elvis did not last long. He was hauled into a judge's chambers in August following an afternoon show in Jacksonville, Florida and told that he must tone down his act or the remaining performances would be cancelled. "I can't figure out what I'm doing wrong," Elvis complained. "I know my mother approves of what I'm doing." Nevertheless, he stood still during the subsequent shows; merely extending his little finger to wiggle it provocatively at the audience. Needless to say, the crowd went wild. The next day in New Orleans, Elvis gave full expression to his pent-up gyrations, giving an uninhibited performance that threatened to demolish the stage.

Within weeks, Elvis was in Hollywood playing his first film role in *Love Me Tender*. He took a break from filming on Sunday, September 9 to make his first appearance on the *Ed Sullivan Show*. A slot on the prestigious Sullivan show marked the pinnacle of any entertainer's career; it meant that he had arrived. Elvis made his appearance via live remote from the CBS Studios in Los Angeles. Over 80 per cent of the viewing audience tuned in to watch him perform 'Don't Be Cruel', 'Love Me Tender', 'Ready Teddy', and a portion of 'Hound Dog'.

The media responded by running a statement from the San Diego Police Chief, warning that he would jail Elvis for disorderly conduct if he returned to the city with a repeat of his performance from earlier that year.

All the hoopla surrounding Elvis' first film role drove advance sales of the soundtrack album to *Love Me Tender* through the roof. The album was certified gold before it was even released. *Variety*, the bible of the entertainment industry, declared "Elvis a millionaire in one year." Exactly one year previous, Elvis had been playing dates at county fairs and small town high school gyms in places most people had never heard of, and where most people had never heard of him. Twelve months later, there was hardly a person alive in the civilised world who had not heard of Elvis Presley.

A return appearance on the *Ed Sullivan Show* on October 28 featured Elvis performing live from New York City. The play-list was nearly an exact repeat of the September show, with the exception of substituting 'Love Me' in the place of 'Ready Teddy'. Earlier that day, the unveiling of a 40-foot tall cut-out of Elvis on the Times Square Paramount Theater advertised the imminent premiere of *Love Me Tender*, which was about to undergo some unexpected last-minute modification.

Elvis was hurriedly booked into a local film studio the next day to shoot a new ending for the movie. Preview audiences had reacted badly to the onscreen demise of their idol, yet the death of character Johnny Reno formed an important plot point that could not be changed. A solution was found by superimposing a ghostly image of Elvis over the closing scene of his character's burial, singing a reprise of the title song. Those who looked closely might have noticed that the ghost sported Elvis' trademark dyed black hair, whereas Johnny wore Elvis' natural blond colour.

The following day, trade papers reported that sales of Elvis' singles had topped the 10 million mark, accounting for nearly two-thirds of the RCA label's total record sales for the year since his signing.

1957

The year began with a third and final appearance on the *Ed Sullivan Show*, featuring the infamous performance of 'Don't Be Cruel' that deleted Elvis from the waist down. His rendition of the classic 'Peace In The Valley' was filmed full length, however, marking for many fans the first indication of Elvis' life-long love of gospel music.

Two days later, the Memphis draft board celebrated Elvis' twenty-second birthday by holding a press conference to announce that he had been classified 1-A, making it likely that he would be drafted in the next six to eight months. Elvis left Memphis the following day for Hollywood, to begin pre-production on the film *Loving You*.

He returned in March to put a $1,000 deposit on Graceland, an 18-acre estate on the outskirts of town, with the purchase being finalised the following week for $102,500. Presenting his parents with the deed to the mansion was one of Elvis' proudest moments. He had long dreamed of installing his mother in the palace that he felt she deserved. Elvis had definite ideas about how he wanted to live and immediately began refurbishing the place along more modern lines, but those who knew the elegance of its former decoration thought the new décor to be in somewhat dubious taste.

A performance in Chicago at the end of the month marked the debut of the iconic gold leaf suit that became inextricably linked to Elvis' image in the early phase of his career. Ironically, given his predilection for flashy stage attire, Elvis was embarrassed by the suit and afterward usually only wore the jacket. The tour ended on a sour note with the cancellation of a Canadian show due to pressure from religious groups, and Elvis being pelted with eggs on the tour's closing date in Philadelphia. Apparently, not all the citizens of "The City of Brotherly Love" loved Elvis.

Celebrity and the barrage of criticism it invited weighed heavily on the young performer. A conversation with a Memphis minister following Easter Sunday services gives insight into the pressures Elvis was under at the time: "I am the most miserable young man you have ever seen," he complained. "I have got more money than I can ever spend, I have thousands of fans out there, and I have a lot of people who call themselves my friends, but I am miserable."

Elvis stayed in town just long enough to see the famous music note gates installed at Graceland, before heading back to Hollywood to begin filming *Jailhouse Rock*. A performance in Los Angeles late in October scandalised local and national press, and provoked outrage from an audience largely made up of Hollywood celebrities and their children. The Los Angeles Vice Squad threatened Elvis with jail time if the show was not cleaned up, and the next evening's performance was much restrained.

A November 11 show for military families stationed at Pearl Harbor, Hawaii was Elvis' final public performance before entering the army. Unbeknownst to him, with the exception of a rare charity benefit, it would also be his last live public performance until 1969.

The year ended on a sombre note with the long-anticipated announcement that a draft notice was imminent. All branches of the armed forces except for the marines had made bids for Elvis' services, offering tours of duty as an entertainer and public relations spokesman. Elvis selected the army because he wanted to serve his country as an ordinary soldier, although Colonel Parker's planned publicity campaign made that a near impossibility.

1958

Parker applied for and was granted a deferment until March in order to allow his client to meet the contractual obligation to film *King Creole*. Spending the night before his induction with family and close friends, Elvis admitted privately his fear that his whole career was coming to an end; that the fans would forget him while he was away. The following day, Elvis reported to the draft board for processing, officially entering military service on March 24, 1958. The hoopla surrounding Elvis' army induction was later portrayed in the thinly veiled Broadway play and subsequent hit film *Bye, Bye Birdie.*

After completing basic training at Fort Hood, Texas in June, Elvis was granted a brief furlough, some of which was spent in an all-night recording session in Nashville. It would be his last for two years. The resulting cuts were far fewer than what had been hoped for, but provided some of the backlog of singles that helped keep Elvis' career alive during his remaining tour of duty.

Gladys had been feeling ill all that summer. With Elvis slated to complete tank training in just a few days, his parents were finally convinced to return to Memphis early so that Gladys could see her regular doctor. She made it back to Graceland, only to be rushed to the hospital the following day, where it was determined that she was suffering from a previously undiagnosed liver ailment.

When Elvis found out, he was frantic with worry. He applied for emergency leave, but was denied. Colonel Parker's intervention in Washington, DC finally got the seven-day leave granted, sparing Elvis the consequences of going AWOL, as he had threatened. He arrived in Memphis on August 13, racing immediately to a tearful reunion with his mother, who died the following day. The funeral, originally planned to be held at Graceland, was moved to the funeral home at the last minute when security was deemed inadequate. Both Elvis and his father nearly collapsed at several points during the service, and Elvis was inconsolable at the cemetery. Parker negotiated an extension of leave so that his client could pull himself together. Before leaving Graceland to return to Fort Hood, Elvis left instructions that

Gladys' room was to be preserved just as she had left it.

In September, Elvis was assigned to the Third Armoured Division based in Friedberg, Germany. Vernon, Grandma Minnie Mae, and an entourage of friends prepared to move to Germany for the duration. At the departure press conference held alongside the USS Randall, Colonel Parker staged Elvis' farewell for the press, which was repeated eight times as Elvis walked up the ship's gangplank and waved to the photographers. A final press conference was held in Germany at the former Nazi barracks that housed the US Army troops, during which Elvis publicly expressed his concern that his fans would forget him during his military service. Once the press questions were concluded, Private Elvis Presley was declared off-limits to journalists. 'One Night With You', released that month, became the biggest selling single since 'Jailhouse Rock' the year before.

1959

Colonel Parker shifted his media machine into high gear. Throughout the year, he launched a constant stream of statements to the press: keeping them abreast of the latest film negotiations, orchestrating "candid" photo sessions and telephone interviews from Elvis' private off-base residence, and arranging for publicity photos of Elvis lending his support to international charitable causes. Parker even managed to rein in RCA, convincing the label to ration out its precious backlog of Elvis recordings, releasing new singles and compilation albums of previous releases at regular 20-week intervals. And when Elvis was promoted to Private First Class, Specialist Fourth Class, Parker made sure that everyone in the press knew about it.

What Parker did not want the press to find out about was

the budding relationship between his 29-year-old client and a 14-year-old army brat named Priscilla Beaulieu. The two had met in September at a party held at Elvis' home in Germany and had quickly become inseparable. The press finally got wind of the romance when Priscilla appeared at the airstrip for Elvis' send-off. Photographs of her bearing the caption "The girl he left behind" tipped off the public to the relationship. Fortunately for all involved, the photos made Priscilla look older than her actual age. It had not been that long since the career of rocker Jerry Lee Lewis had evaporated overnight because of a similar relationship with an underage girl.

1960

A newly promoted Acting Sergeant Elvis Presley commented on his military service in an interview several weeks before his return to the United States: "People were expecting me to mess up; to goof up. They thought I couldn't take it, and I was determined to go to any limits to prove otherwise."

Sergeant Presley departed Germany in March 1960 for processing at Fort Dix, New Jersey, prior to discharge several days later. A press conference held at Graceland marked the return of Elvis to civilian life and the beginning of Parker's long planned-for campaign to jumpstart his client's flagging career. Elvis visited his mother's grave to see the marker and statuary that had been installed while he was away, and caught up with friends before heading to Nashville for his first recording session in nearly two years. The session came none too soon, as RCA had by then completely exhausted its backlog of unreleased recordings, and taken to offering a series of "greatest hits" albums which had not been big sellers. The all-night session yielded the single 'Stuck on You', which was raced into production and released 48 hours later. The song reached number one in the charts within a month.

Then it was off to Florida to tape a television appearance with Frank Sinatra that would be broadcast in May. The pairing of Frank Sinatra with Elvis Presley was a strange one, as Sinatra had very publicly denounced rock'n'roll as music "for cretinous goons", but he was impressed with Elvis' sincerity: "I get the feeling he really believes in what he's doing." Perhaps as a result of the Sinatra influence, Elvis' entourage of pals – dubbed the Memphis Mafia by the press – began wearing the matching sunglasses and dark sharkskin suits favoured by the Rat Pack.

Elvis was back in Nashville for another recording session that produced the classics 'It's Now or Never' and 'Are You Lonesome Tonight?' before heading out to Hollywood to begin work on the comeback film *G.I. Blues*. Despite Elvis' dissatisfaction with the quality of both the songs and the script, *G.I. Blues* became the 14th-highest grossing film of the year.

At the beginning of summer, Vernon Presley married Dee Stanley, a recent divorcee with three young sons. The relationship had begun the previous year in Germany, where Stanley was the then-wife of an army officer. There had been a secret romance, but Elvis was not pleased. He accused Vernon of betraying the memory of his late wife, and never attempted to acknowledge his new step-mother with anything more than polite indifference. The relationship between father and son would soon be mended, but it was not long afterward that Vernon moved out of Graceland and signed over its deed to his angry son.

The summer ended with a return to Hollywood to shoot a

western drama that would undergo several name variations before being titled *Flaming Star*. Initially slated to be a non-musical role, somewhere along the way the picture acquired a few songs, probably at the instigation of Colonel Parker. It was his idea that, with few exceptions, Elvis should release only soundtrack albums tied to his film roles. Even many single releases would eventually be drawn from soundtrack cuts. This might not have been such a bad idea if Elvis was still being offered quality material to record. A-list songwriters – those with a history of producing hit material – who had worked with Elvis in the past refused Parker's new demand that they share writing credit and half the royalties in return for his client recording their songs. As a result, Elvis was being offered mediocre material that not even a star of his prodigious talent was capable of improving. The songs chosen for *Flaming Star* were a particular embarrassment to Elvis. He begged that they not be released on an album and, in fact, only two of them ended up being used in the final film.

Perhaps in response, Elvis went back into the studio to record the music that he truly loved. *His Hand In Mine* was his first album devoted to gospel music, and revealed a fully realised display of singing ability that had previously only been hinted at during his final pre-military television performance. The album sold moderately well in its initial release, but went on to become a back stock success for the singer.

Elvis was back in Hollywood again in November to film *Wild In The Country*. Despite a promising script and the expectation that this would finally be the serious acting role he had long been hoping for, Elvis was once again disappointed. When audience response to *Flaming Star* proved lukewarm, the studio panicked and decided to throw a few songs into the new film. The disappointment Elvis must have felt shows in his performance, which also betrays the effects of the amphetamine habit he had acquired in the army to help him stay awake on guard duty.

Elvis hated street drugs, but prescription drugs were a completely different matter. He saw nothing wrong in using drugs prescribed by a doctor. The problem was that he had doctors in Memphis and doctors in Los Angeles, all prescribing various diet and sleeping pills without knowledge of what the others were doing. Film studios were notorious at the time for handing out "uppers" to keep their stars energised during long working hours. For a man with chronic insomnia and a restless nature, amphetamine abuse was almost inevitable. He could sleep all day and play all night whenever he had a break between movies, but while a film was being shot, Elvis needed pills to wake up and more pills to put him to sleep. In the Hollywood of the 1960s, this was considered normal.

Like many entertainers, Elvis came alive at night, which is part of the reason why he and Las Vegas would later prove to be such a perfect fit. He preferred evening recording sessions that could stretch into the following morning. He loved late night movies, but in a typically idiosyncratic style. Several times a week, whenever Elvis was in Memphis, he hired the local movie theatre after regular hours to privately screen his favourite films. Some nights he and a few friends might view three or four pictures in a row, or watch one of Elvis' particular favourites over and over. Other times he would quickly grow bored and be ready to leave after only a few minutes.

During the summer months, a favoured late night pastime was for the gang to pile into their cars and drive out to the Memphis fairgrounds. Elvis rented the Fairgrounds Amusement Park after midnight so that he and the gang could ride the pippin and crash the dodgem cars into each other. The fun often continued long past daybreak. Judging from the quantity of Cokes and coffee charged to Elvis' account, not all of the guests found it as easy to stay awake as did their host. This pattern of night time activity had begun early on in his career, and continued for the remainder of his life.

1961

January 1961 began a busy period for Elvis, starting with the signing of a four-picture deal with Paramount Studios, and the contractual guarantee of an additional four films with MGM. The pattern established on his previous films now became standard. Work on each production began with a soundtrack recording session, followed by two to three weeks of principle filming and a week of overdubs.

Although he made an effort in the beginning, Elvis grew more dissatisfied with each picture he made. The songs selected for him were increasingly inane, the scripts uniformly weak, and the roles virtually identical. All that changed was the leading lady. The longer it went on, the more creatively frustrated Elvis became. He was the sort of person who needed constant stimulation and activity. He wanted to be the best at everything he did, and he was convinced that he could achieve a level of proficiency faster than the average man.

But in the absence of a challenge, Elvis was inclined to be lazy. Had he been given acting roles that required him to stretch his abilities, he may have been inclined to take acting lessons, or learn more about the technical side of the film industry. As things stood, the roles Elvis was given barely required him to do anything more than just be himself, and he certainly did not need to be told how to act like Elvis Presley.

So why did Elvis continue to accept acting roles he

disliked? Why did he agree to record songs he felt no affinity for? Why did he discontinue live performances, when onstage was where Elvis burned hottest and brightest? There is no simple answer, but it had to do with his business arrangement with Colonel Parker. Parker made the decisions and his client delivered the goods. Elvis was the product; Parker was the salesman: they needed each other, whether they liked it or not.

And what a product! There had never been a star like Elvis Presley before. There had never been an entertainer with the raw sexual energy that he exuded. Style, charisma, the ability to reach the individual in the crowd; no other performer had the physical power and presence that Elvis had onstage. Just as Elvis was the first of his kind, so was Colonel Parker the first of his. Only he had ever marketed a star of that calibre; only he had the vision to build that kind of career. Other "star-makers" came later, some of them much better skilled, but they all learned from Parker. At the time, there was no one else who could have represented Elvis. There was only one Colonel.

Colonel Parker had early on discovered that films held an incredible money-making potential. Not only for his client, but also – perhaps especially so – for him. In addition to his manager's commission, there was a host of side deals that could be made, as well as signing bonuses, profit participation, and consultation fees. Then there were the soundtrack recordings, which Parker artfully negotiated so that he was getting paid by both the film studio *and* the record label for the same record. Each movie contract was a gold strike, and Parker mined it for all it was worth. He made sure that Elvis got his share too, but over time that share dwindled down until it was Parker who was taking home the bigger pay cheque.

Films were also easy money. An Elvis movie could be churned out with a minimum of cost, so that both the studio and the star were assured of making money. Touring, in contrast, was expensive and exhausting. A large percentage of the profits got eaten up with travel costs, venue rentals, and salaries for musicians and crew. As long as the fans were willing to pay for movie tickets and soundtrack albums, Parker saw no reason to have to work harder for his money than he had to.

The first picture made under the new contracts was Paramount's *Blue Hawaii*. While Elvis may not have been altogether happy with the role, the film turned out to be one of his best. The soundtrack album was one of the best as well, featuring the classic 'Can't Help Falling In Love'. It sold two million copies in the first two months, reached number one in the charts, and went on to sell more copies during Elvis' lifetime than any of his other recordings. The next films, *Follow That Dream* and *Kid Galahad*, did not perform as well.

1962

Film role followed upon film role in quick succession – *Girls! Girls! Girls!, It Happened At The World's Fair* – each becoming more formulaic as time went on. A break came in the summer, when Elvis convinced Priscilla's father to allow her to come to Los Angeles for a two-week visit. She returned in December to spend the Christmas holiday at Graceland, sleeping through the first 48 hours of the visit due to the strength of the sleeping pills Elvis had given her. After promising appropriate chaperones and living arrangements, Elvis succeeded in charming Priscilla's parents into allowing their daughter to finish her schooling in the United States. He arranged for Priscilla to complete her senior year at Immaculate Heart High School in Memphis.

1963

Elvis spent the beginning of the year travelling between Memphis and Hollywood, where he was filming *Fun In Acapulco*. Priscilla graduated high school in May but, fearing his attendance would disrupt the proceedings, asked Elvis to stay away.

That summer, Priscilla stayed behind at Graceland while Elvis left for Hollywood to begin filming *Viva Las Vegas*. Rumours soon began to fly about a possible relationship with co-star Ann-Margret, which Elvis categorically denied in nightly telephone conversations with a worried Priscilla. When photographs finally confirmed the rumour, Priscilla was furious. She stormed into Los Angeles prepared to confront Elvis about the relationship, but was hastily sent back to Memphis.

A quote from Ann-Margret – then in London for the premiere of her breakthrough film *Bye, Bye Birdie* – had recently appeared in the press, stating that she loved Elvis, but did not know whether they would marry. The news caused such a commotion that it was thought prudent to remove the still teenage Priscilla to a more secluded location, just in case the press started snooping around. The ensuing publicity blitz surrounding Ann-Margret made Colonel Parker fear that she would upstage Elvis in his own movie. At Parker's instigation, two of the three duets the two stars had filmed together were dropped from *Viva Las Vegas*.

Whether the quote was accurate or not, the relationship between Elvis and Ann-Margret was doomed from the start. She wanted a career and he wanted a wife who was at his beck and call. The two continued to see each other off and on for some time after their film pairing ended, but managed to do so outside the prying gaze of the press.

Despite the financial success of his movies, studio executives were not completely satisfied. Following the filming of *Kissin' Cousins*, they complained about Elvis' weight, and strongly suggested that he get back in shape for his next picture. The fans, however, did not seem to notice. December ended with Elvis listed in industry trade papers as Hollywood's seventh-biggest money-making actor for that year.

1964

There have been several key events in music history. Elvis had instigated one in 1957, which took rock'n'roll to the masses. Another came in 1964, when The Beatles made their American debut on the Ed Sullivan Show. While few recognised it at the time, the British Invasion was about to sweep aside many of the performers who had defined rock'n'roll. Elvis sent a telegram which was read during the broadcast, welcoming The Beatles to America and wishing them well. Over the course of the next few years he would have reason to regret his enthusiasm. As The Beatles' star made its meteoric climb, Elvis' star was being eclipsed. That was still a ways off, though. For the time being, Elvis was still king. *Viva Las Vegas* ended the year at number 10 in box office sales, out-grossing The Beatles' *Hard Day's Night*.

An April newspaper item titled "Elvis Helps in Success of Burton-O'Toole Movie" confirmed what Elvis had suspected for some time: his films were second rate. The article stated that it was the profits from Elvis Presley vehicles that enabled Hollywood producer Hal Wallis to finance first-class epics such as *Becket*, starring serious actors Richard Burton and Peter O'Toole. "In order to do the artistic pictures," Wallis was quoted as saying, "it is necessary to make the commercially successful Presley pictures," adding almost as an afterthought, "but that doesn't mean a Presley picture can't have quality, too."

Although he later half-jokingly asked Wallis when he could expect to get his own *Becket* role, Elvis was deeply hurt. The knowledge that his movies were considered déclassé by the industry, despite their huge financial success, disheartened him. Elvis did the best he could in *Roustabout*, *Girl Happy*, and *Tickle Me* that year, but the scripts did not give him much to work with. Perhaps it was not entirely coincidental that from that point onward, the quality of Elvis' onscreen performances went into a slow decline.

At the time Elvis was feeling most vulnerable, there came an unlikely source of inspiration. It occurred during a haircut when Larry Gellar, a last-minute replacement for Elvis' regular hairdresser, happened to mention his interest in spiritual studies. As Gellar worked, his explanation of spiritual matters seemed to provide answers to questions that Elvis had struggled with for years. "What you're talking about, is what I secretly think about all the time," Elvis confided. "I've always known that there had to be a purpose for my life. I mean, there's got to be a reason," he continued, "why I was chosen to be Elvis Presley." The discussion continued for hours, ending only when Gellar agreed to work for Elvis full time. In the months that followed he became Elvis' closest confidant and advisor, to the growing resentment and displeasure of Colonel Parker and the Memphis Mafia.

The next day, Gellar brought copies of the books he had mentioned, which Elvis read voraciously; underlining favourite passages and making notations in the margins. He devoted most of the next two months to intensive study and spiritual discussion with Gellar, often at the expense of other obligations. The situation began to unravel when Parker, frustrated by several missed recording sessions, accused his client of being on a religious kick. "My life is not a kick," Elvis retorted. "It's real."

Not only was it real, but music, religion and life were pretty much synonymous in Elvis' mind. The Presleys had been church-going people since before Elvis was born. Gladys' uncle Gains Mansell had been the family's pastor for many years, and Elvis' first exposure to music had been the hymns and gospel songs he heard sung in the First Assembly of God church in East Tupelo, Mississippi.

Elvis had first been drawn to gospel music as a child, and he had not had to look hard to find it. It was everywhere: at church, at home, on the radio, at weekend community sings and summer tent revival meetings. It was the smooth, four-part harmonies of white gospel quartets and the soaring, soul-cleansing praise of coloured gospel choirs. Elvis loved both styles and incorporated them into his own recordings, both sacred and profane. In a way, he did not see much of a difference between the two. He attacked rock'n'roll with evangelical fervour, and sang gospel in a sultry, bluesy drawl. To separate one from the other would have seemed unthinkable.

Never one to do things by halves, whenever Elvis found a new interest, he pursued it to an almost obsessive degree. At the moment the interest was spiritual. He delved into Eastern philosophy, especially the writings of Daya Mata. He attended the Self Realization Fellowship retreat to learn the benefits of meditation.

During the course of his studies, Elvis added a Jewish "chai" to the cross he wore on a chain around his neck, and a Star of David to his mother's grave marker. This may have been a response to a broadened spiritual awareness, or to "hedge his bets" as he claimed. Or it may have stemmed from the little-known fact that his maternal grandmother was Jewish. Whatever the reason, these were all parts of a larger scene that was driving those around Elvis to distraction.

Parker feared this "religious kick" would alienate the fans and interfere with current and future profit potential. Priscilla found herself in fourth place behind this all-consuming new interest, Larry Gellar, and Elvis' stable of pals. As for them, they were sick of Elvis' endless discussion and quotation from the growing pile of spiritual books Gellar regularly supplied. They deeply resented his influence and took every opportunity to let Gellar know it. Whether the antagonism was kept hidden from Elvis, or his devotion to study made him oblivious, or whether he simply chose to ignore it, the situation was quickly building to a head.

Meanwhile, Colonel Parker had achieved a long sought-after dream of his own. Besides a contract for Elvis to appear in two movies for United Artists, Parker negotiated another three-picture deal with MGM. The MGM contract finally put him in the elite cadre of managers capable of putting together a deal worth $1,000,000.

1965

1965 was the year Elvis turned 30 years old, but not much else changed. The drudgery of soundtrack recording sessions and film shoots continued unabated through the year, and it became increasingly obvious that Elvis no longer cared about either. Trite songs and poor production values had made his movies an embarrassment to him, but he was trapped. *Harum Scarum*, *Frankie And Johnny*, *Paradise, Hawaiian Style*; some were better than others, but none of them were great. It seemed that as long as the films made money for the studios, everyone but Elvis was going to be happy.

More and more Elvis sought ways to distract himself, which usually meant spending profligate amounts of money. He bought motorcycles by the dozen, built the Meditation Garden on the grounds at Graceland, and embarked on a mania for slot-car racing. Eventually the extensive track was housed in a specially constructed building next to the pool patio, now known as the "Trophy Room".

The one bright spot of the year was the release of 'Crying In The Chapel', which rose to number three in the US charts and number one in Great Britain. It was Elvis' first Top 10 single in two years, and in many ways the lyrics were a reflection of his own personal search for peace of mind. That the single temporarily wrested the top spot from The Beatles, who had virtually owned the American charts for the past year, must have been a source of some satisfaction. When their respective managers arranged for the Fab Four to meet the King at his Los Angeles home later in the year, he all but ignored them. The visit ended after several uncomfortable hours of half-hearted attempts at conversation.

The remaining singles and albums Elvis released that year performed poorly. Sales had declined, as they had for many American pop singers, and new artists like Bob Dylan were capturing the public's attention.

1966

Filming began on *Spinout* in January, followed by *Double Trouble*. With only one movie of their original three-picture agreement released, MGM extended the deal to include an additional four films. Another contract was negotiated in

April for one more picture with Hal Wallis, *Easy Come, Easy Go*, which proved to be the last time Elvis worked with the producer.

Perhaps inspired by the success of the previous year's 'Crying In The Chapel', Elvis chose to record an album of gospel music. Unlike the film soundtrack albums of which he had grown weary, and whose recording sessions he dreaded, Elvis was anxious to begin work on this new project. He arrived promptly on time for each of the all-night sessions and quickly achieved the desired results. As a group, the finished recordings represented part of the body of work that Elvis was most proud of. RCA was pleased too, and announced their intention to extend their recording contract with Elvis through December 1974. The album *How Great Thou Art* was released the following February to tepid sales, but the effort was rewarded with a 1967 Grammy Award for Best Sacred Performance. It was Elvis' first Grammy win.

Near the end of the year, Elvis became interested in horse-back riding; an interest which quickly took over his life. His Christmas gift to Priscilla that year was a horse, but the biggest surprise happened a few days earlier when Elvis proposed marriage.

1967

The year began with a five-week spending spree. When it was over, Elvis had purchased 30 horses, an immense quantity of riding gear, and a Mississippi ranch he renamed the Circle-G. Land behind Graceland was cleared to build a riding area and stables were ordered built, but the facility was outgrown before it was even completed. Elvis moved to the Circle-G, taking with him his gang of pals and the bulk of the herd. As more and more of the gang arrived, the ranch house, too, was quickly outgrown. A program of extensive (and expensive) remodelling and additions ensued, along with the purchase of dozens of pickup trucks.

With Colonel Parker negotiating new film contracts before the old ones were completed, Elvis saw himself trapped in a series of stale acting roles that he feared might never end. He dreaded having to face another hack script and even worse songs, and the next picture – *Clambake* – was the worst one yet. Hollywood was a world away from life at the Circle-G, and the longer he stayed there, the harder it was to think about leaving.

By the beginning of March, Elvis had several times failed to report for work on his next film. Finally, Colonel Parker stepped in. Elvis soon left for Hollywood, but two days after arriving, he fell in the bathroom of his Los Angeles home. The resulting concussion delayed production another 11 days.

Parker was furious, and used the situation to lay down the law. He read Elvis the riot act, fired members of the Memphis Mafia he deemed disloyal, banished Larry Gellar and any further talk of spiritualism, and reined in the money being lavished on the Circle-G. It was probably on this occasion that a wedding date was set for Elvis and Priscilla. Rumours of the marriage appeared in the press the day after the filming of *Clambake* was completed.

The May 1st wedding, as orchestrated by Parker, took on a side-show quality. The actual ceremony was held just before noon in a private suite at the Aladdin Hotel in Las Vegas, after which the couple was immediately whisked to a press conference in a downstairs ballroom. The reception that followed was staged for the press as more of a publicity stunt than a nuptial celebration, with the newly-weds, their family and guests herded into different configurations for the photographers. Four weeks later, the couple again donned their wedding attire for a private reception held at Graceland. Within two weeks, Priscilla learned that she was pregnant.

The remainder of the year was primarily spent filming *Speedway* and *Stay Away, Joe*, and on recording their respective soundtrack albums. Elvis and Priscilla returned to Graceland for the Christmas holiday, where they remained until the birth of their daughter. The passion for horseback riding that had consumed Elvis' attention at the beginning of the year was largely forgotten by then. With remodelling underway at Graceland in preparation for the upcoming birth, the ranch was shut down and the dispersal of its equipment began.

Graceland was the family home, where Grandma Minnie and Aunt Delta lived, but Elvis and Priscilla seldom stayed there, except for Christmas visits. Most of their time was now spent in California, shuttling between a succession of houses in Bel Air and Palm Springs. Like cars, motorcycles and everything else, Elvis bought new ones frequently.

1968

News of the million-dollar deal Colonel Parker negotiated for an NBC TV Christmas Special was quickly eclipsed by the February 1 birth of Lisa Marie Presley. Three weeks later the family moved into their new Los Angeles home. Filming of *Live A Little, Love A Little* was well underway when RCA released the single 'You'll Never Walk Alone' in time for Easter. Elvis was nominated for another Best Sacred Performance Grammy Award, but lost out to former Statesman lead singer Jake Hess.

With filming completed, Parker organised a series of

Christmas Special planning sessions with executives from the NBC network and the show's sponsor, the Singer Sewing Machine Company. When Elvis voiced his desire to do something completely different from his film work, the special began to evolve in a new direction. Parker backed off when it came to the creative side of the project, as usual allowing Elvis final say over the material. The Colonel's only stipulation was that since he had originally contracted for a Christmas Special, the show had to include at least one Christmas song. Director Steve Binder was brought in to work up a script while Elvis took his family on vacation in Hawaii.

By the time Elvis returned to Los Angles in June, the special had turned into a sort of musical autobiography, held together by the universal theme of man's quest to find happiness. Elvis loved it. The assassination of presidential hopeful Robert Kennedy in Los Angeles just days later sparked the idea of incorporating an anti-prejudice social message, which galvanised the production and climaxed in the show-stopping closing number 'If I Can Dream'.

Rehearsals began in the middle of the month and continued for 10 days. Elvis was emotionally involved in the project to a degree he had not experienced in many years. The creative energy of the process both excited and rejuvenated him, and reinforced his desire to break free of the career rut he felt trapped in.

As the scheduled start date for filming drew closer, Elvis began to worry. The script included an acoustic segment to be shot in two sessions in front of an on-camera studio audience. Elvis had not performed in front of a live audience in over 10 years, and wondered if they would still respond to him. When the day arrived to film the segment, Elvis was a nervous wreck and doubted whether he could go through with it. He sweated so much during the first session that the black leather suit he wore had to be dried out and reshaped before filming could resume. As it turned out, Elvis need not have worried; his performance was electrifying.

Filming continued for another three days, culminating in the special's closing sequence. Dressed in a double-breasted white suit and backed by his name in 10-foot lighted letters, Elvis poured his heart into the song that had been written specifically for this segment. 'If I Can Dream' was taped five times, the intensity building with each performance until Elvis had transformed the number into a gospel anthem.

After resting for a week, Elvis reported for work on his next film, a Western that would ultimately be titled *Charro!* Although initially envisioned as a gritty dramatic role, MGM decided after viewing the rough cut to have Elvis record a title song. Within days he was back at work on another MGM film, *The Trouble With Girls*.

Throughout the fall, Colonel Parker kept a close eye on the editing of the NBC special. After viewing a rough cut of the show, he fired off a memo complaining about the lack of a Christmas song – his one request, per the contract. Threatened with failure to fulfil their obligation, NBC replaced a steamy dance number with an extraneous version of 'Blue Christmas'. The completed show was broadcast at the beginning of December, and pulled in the network's highest ratings numbers of the year. The vast majority of reviews called the show an unqualified success, and raved about its star. What began as a simple seasonal offering became unofficially known as the Comeback Special.

On the heels of the NBC show, offers for more television appearances poured in, but Parker had bigger plans. He capitalised on his client's recent success by negotiating a four-week summer engagement at the International Hotel in

Las Vegas for the following year, securing Elvis an unheard of $10,000 a week.

1969

Elvis began the year determined to put an end to the long string of insipid soundtrack albums that had been released in the past. For his upcoming recording session, the decision was made to forgo the RCA studio in Nashville in favour of a studio closer to home. Elvis' producer agreed that the switch might spark a new sound. The January sessions held at the American Studio in Memphis yielded the best songs of Elvis' latter career, and continued in February after a two-week break. The album *From Elvis In Memphis* topped out in the charts at number 13, with the singles 'In The Ghetto', 'Suspicious Minds', and 'Kentucky Rain' hitting number three, number one, and number 16 respectively. 'Suspicious Minds' was Elvis' first number one release since 1962, as well as his last.

The last – but not worst – of Elvis' feature films, *A Change Of Habit*, began filming in March. When it was completed, he returned to Graceland.

With new music and a new attitude in place, Elvis decided he also needed a new look for his upcoming Las Vegas debut. He called upon NBC costume designer Bill Belew for ideas. The results continued the high "Napoleon" collars Belew first introduced in the NBC special, a look favoured by Elvis for disguising the length of his neck. The Vegas stage costumes included a number of innovations that became trademarks: the elaborate hip belts, chest-baring necklines, and long silk scarves.

Work on the act began in earnest in July, as Elvis finalised the arrangements of the songs he wanted to use. He contacted nearly every musician he had ever worked with in his search to assemble the band that would back him up onstage. He also hired a male gospel quartet, the Imperials, and a black female soul group called the Sweet Inspirations to provide background vocals. Rehearsals began in Las Vegas in the middle of the month, two weeks before the engagement was set to start. On opening night, July 31st, Elvis stood backstage battling a severe case of stage fright while he waited for his cue to enter. This was the first time he had ever attempted to perform a full one-hour live show.

Elvis paused onstage for just a second before tearing into a searing rendition of 'Blue Suede Shoes' that had the celebrity-filled audience jumping to its feet. Elvis catapulted across the stage from one number to the next, driving the audience wild until the reaction recalled the screaming pandemonium of his early years.

With the audience inside threatening to tear down the showroom walls, Parker hurriedly wrote out a new contract on a coffee shop tablecloth that guaranteed $1,000,000 for two four-week engagements per year, to run for five years. Worth a total of $5,000,000, excluding merchandising and the usual side deals, it was the biggest score that Parker had pulled off yet. His deal commissions now ranged up to a whopping 50 per cent.

The record-breaking engagement took in over $1,500,000. RCA recorded the performances for a double album entitled *From Memphis To Vegas/From Vegas To Memphis*, which was released in October. It was during the run of the show that the first intimations began leaking to the press that Elvis' marriage was in trouble.

With the Las Vegas engagement completed, Elvis had time on his hands that he was at a loss to know how to fill. For the first time in nearly 10 years there was no film set or recording studio to report to. Elvis travelled restlessly from place to place for the next few months, unable to find a spot that suited him. He landed back at Graceland just before Christmas, still unable to relax for long.

1970

The new decade brought with it a desire for more contemporary musical relevance. Elvis spent the beginning of January working up new material for his Vegas act. The push for new songs stemmed from the fact that the shows were once again to be recorded for a live album. Along with 'Proud Mary', 'Polk Salad Annie' and 'Walk A Mile In My Shoes', Elvis included oldies like 'Release Me', 'See See Rider', and 'The Wonder Of You'.

It was not only the music that changed. This Vegas engagement marked the first appearance of the jumpsuits and mutton-chop sideburns Elvis wore throughout the remainder of his career. New onstage choreography incorporated karate movements, a reflection of Elvis' long-standing interest in the sport.

Once again, the Vegas shows drew rave reviews. Elvis left immediately afterward to perform two shows a day for three days at the Houston Astrodome. The turnout for the first show was disappointing, making Elvis wonder whether he was capable of drawing a crowd outside Las Vegas. However, the second show and those thereafter set new attendance records for the venue. At a press conference following the final show, Elvis accepted gold records for five of his 1969 recordings. He also received an honorary gold deputy's badge from the Houston sheriff, which touched off a mania for collecting police badges that continued for the next few years.

Five nights of recording sessions began in June, this time

scheduled at RCA's Nashville studio. Unlike many of the film soundtrack sessions, where Elvis would show up late (if he showed up at all) and spend hours singing gospel songs with his back-up singers – anything to forestall having to face the loathsome movie songs – he was now anxious to get back into the studio again. He came prepared to work and quickly ran through the stack of songs that had been selected for the sessions.

In contrast to material he did not care about, which sometimes required upwards of 30 takes before getting one good performance, these songs were captured after very few tries. When music publishing company representatives had nothing left to offer, Elvis started to work up a series of favourite country tunes that later formed the basis of the concept album *Elvis Country*. The sessions ended with 35 masters completed.

Rehearsals for the summer Vegas shows began in mid-July. Colonel Parker had put together a deal with MGM for a behind-the-scenes documentary to be titled *That's The Way It Is* for release in November. The rehearsals and upcoming shows were planned and filmed with that use in mind.

During the run of the engagement, the International Hotel's security office was tipped off to a plot to kidnap Elvis, which prompted the addition of additional security staff. A second phone call was placed to a member of Elvis' staff, demanding $50,000 in return for identifying an individual who intended to assassinate the star during that evening's show. The threat was deemed serious enough to bring in the FBI and hire a crew of private bodyguards. Additionally, Elvis called in many of the former Memphis Mafia, from whom he had become estranged. During the show, security officers were prominently placed throughout the showroom, and a doctor and ambulance stood by backstage. Elvis performed that night with a handgun hidden in each of his boots. The show went off without a hitch and the threats stopped.

A six-day, six-city tour was launched in September to test the viability of large-scale concert tours. The shows were well received, but left Elvis tired, irritable and a day late for a recording session scheduled in Nashville. He arrived in the evening and quickly pushed through the session, completing in six hours the songs required to finish off the country album.

Part of the reason that Elvis was anxious to get through the recording session was that he was due in Memphis to receive an official Shelby County deputy sheriff badge, which conferred the right to carry a pistol. The kidnap threat in Vegas had changed a pastime for collecting honorary badges into a mania for collecting the real thing. This was exceeded only by a concurrent mania for guns. Elvis bought them by the dozen, sometimes having jewellers refit special favourites with gold handle grips.

The success of the first tour assured that there would be more. Parker made arrangements through promoters Concerts West for eight shows to be performed in November at major metropolitan coliseums and arenas. The shows broke attendance records throughout the tour. Parker's cut on tour dates was one-third of the total profits.

Around this time, Elvis ordered a group of gold pendants as gifts for his entourage. The design, as sketched out by he and Priscilla, featured the letters TCB (Taking Care of Business) over a lightning bolt. A female version was designed a few months later that featured the letters TLC (Tender Loving Care). The pendants became coveted souvenirs among his celebrity friends.

Elvis began to show signs of stress as the November tour wound down. His marriage was in trouble, the kidnap threat still plagued his thoughts, and an ongoing paternity suit was headed to court. Elvis ignored Parker's attempts to contact him and did what he always did when he felt under pressure: he spent money. He had his Mercedes fitted out like a patrol car, with flashing blue lights, a police band radio and an arsenal of weaponry. He bought guns in an almost frenzied manner, spending tens of thousands of dollars at a time. He made large donations to police organisations in Tennessee and California. When his father voiced concern about the extravagant sums of money being spent, Elvis responded in typical fashion by purchasing a Mercedes for him.

The obsession with law enforcement paraphernalia hit its peak when Elvis learned that an acquaintance had been awarded a Federal Bureau of Narcotics and Dangerous Drugs badge in acknowledgement of undercover work for the agency. The crusade to procure one of the badges consumed all of Elvis' attention. The opportunity came in the middle of December, in a bizarre three-day episode that stretched credibility.

The adventure began with a flight from Memphis to Washington DC, where Elvis checked into a hotel, then almost immediately checked out and returned to the airport to catch another flight to Los Angeles. He called ahead during a refuelling stop in Dallas, alerting his driver to meet him at the Los Angeles airport, but cautioned the man not to tell anyone his whereabouts. By the time the flight arrived, Elvis was in the throes of an allergic rash caused by a reaction between eye infection medicine he was taking and chocolate he had eaten on the airplane. After receiving treatment for the rash on his face and neck, Elvis announced his immediate return to Washington.

On the return flight he met California Senator George Murphy and during their conversation, secured the senator's help in obtaining the Narcotics Bureau badge he wanted.

Elvis wrote out a letter to President Richard Nixon, offering his services in the government's ongoing campaign against illicit drugs, which he personally delivered to the White House upon his arrival. Elvis spent the morning at the Narcotics Bureau, trying to get an appointment with the director, but was refused. Amazingly, a call came from the White House, saying that the President would be available to meet with Elvis in 45 minutes. He raced to pick up the two-man entourage he had brought along, who were stashed at a hotel, then headed for his meeting.

The photograph of the historic occasion shows Elvis dressed as if he were about to go onstage in Vegas, wearing a purple velvet jumpsuit with a matching double-breasted Edwardian jacket draped over his shoulders, two enormous gold medallions hung from heavy chains, and a belt buckle the size of a turkey platter. The groovy King of Rock'n'Roll shook hands with the President of the United States – probably the most uptight leader the nation had ever known – who grinned like a star-struck fan.

Incredibly, the two men hit it off, and when Elvis left town the next day, it was with the coveted Narcotics Bureau badge in hand. His only regret was that he had been unable to meet FBI Director J. Edgar Hoover. The final irony to the affair was that Elvis, suffering from sleep deprivation, the rash, and the medicine prescribed to treat it, scratched and mumbled sleepily throughout the entire meeting. News reporters cynically suggested that it was the effects of withdrawal from the very type of drugs that he was offering to fight against.

1971

The Junior Chamber of Commerce of America selected Elvis as one of its Ten Outstanding Young Men of the Year for

1970. In his acceptance speech, Elvis stated that every dream he had ever dreamed had come true a hundred times. At the beginning of 1971, that certainly appeared to be true. His recordings were back in the charts, his Vegas shows were hugely successful, and his tour dates were drawing record crowds: Elvis had everything he could possibly want. He ended his speech by saying that life was nothing without a song, so he kept on singing. Clearly moved by the honour, Elvis afterward took the award with him wherever he went.

Following his month-long winter engagement in Vegas, Elvis arrived in Nashville with hopes of completing his annual quota of recordings in one marathon week of sessions. The record company wanted enough material to supply single releases and the pop, gospel and Christmas albums it had planned for the year. Elvis, however, had other ideas and launched into a series of folk ballads. After only four songs, the sessions were unexpectedly called off. The eye infection that had caused him trouble in Washington had suddenly become painful. Elvis ended up being hospitalised for treatment of secondary glaucoma. It was six weeks before the sessions resumed.

When Elvis returned to Nashville in the middle of May, it was to work on the Christmas album that RCA was so anxious to release. He was not at all in the mood, despite the decorated Christmas tree, wrapped gifts, and Santa Claus that had been brought in to establish a holiday atmosphere. However, when the first night's session was over, Elvis had completed half of the necessary cuts. The following sessions were not so successful. His attention scattered, Elvis jumped from pop songs to gospel tunes, periodically returning to the folk ballads that had interested him the previous month. The entire week of work produced 30 masters. None of the album projects were finished, but Elvis was. He packed up and headed for home, but was back again in June to complete the sessions.

Parker had booked Elvis to perform for two weeks at the Sahara Tahoe Hotel, beginning at the end of July. The engagement quickly sold out and broke attendance records at the mountain resort. From there, Elvis went immediately to the Las Vegas Hilton (the former International Hotel) for the annual "Elvis Summer Festival". This time the shows were not a success with the critics, but the fans did not notice; they were as enthusiastic as ever. Elvis was tired and ill, being treated for throat problems, and appeared pre-occupied onstage.

His mood brightened significantly when the National Academy of Recording Arts and Sciences presented him with their Lifetime Achievement Award during the run of the Vegas shows. The prestigious award had only been given out five times before – to Bing Crosby, Frank Sinatra, Duke Ellington, Ella Fitzgerald, and Irving Berlin – and the calibre of the previous recipients made it that much more of an honour.

On the strength of the previous year's concert tours, Elvis embarked on a 12-city tour in November that covered New England and the Midwest. It was on this tour that the capes first appeared as part of Elvis' now heavily jewelled stage costumes. The capes proved very effective in the large arena venues where he performed on tour, but were later dropped from his Vegas shows. They proved to be too easy to grab, and more than once Elvis was nearly pulled into the audience by an over-zealous fan.

With tours and shows completed for the year, the family gathered back to Graceland for Christmas as usual. Elvis and Priscilla played the loving couple that they always did in public, but their friends noticed a change in the relationship.

When Priscilla and Lisa Marie prepared to return to Los Angeles before the big New Years Eve party that Elvis traditionally hosted, it was obvious that something was wrong. Once she had departed, Elvis announced that Priscilla was leaving him; that she had not told him why, only that she no longer loved him.

For at least the previous year, Elvis had been juggling relationships with several women. That Priscilla might find out about them, but would turn a blind eye, was expected. What Elvis had not expected was that his wife might grow tired of playing the dutiful wife while he was out playing around. He had once joked that the reason for choosing such a young girl to be his bride was so he could raise her to be what he wanted. What Priscilla became was a woman, with aspirations and needs that went beyond being a mere appendage to her husband's life, something Elvis was not equipped to deal with.

There may have been another, less obvious reason. Elvis' odd devotion to his own mother was such that he put all mothers on a pedestal. Once Priscilla had given birth to their daughter, Elvis mentally moved her from the Wife and Lover category to the Inviolate Madonna category. That was not a situation a woman in her early twenties was likely to find appealing, particularly a woman who was developing a sense of her own identity.

1972

The titles of the new songs Elvis chose for the winter Vegas shows reflected his current mood: 'The Last Time I Saw Her', 'The Sun Ain't Gonna Shine Anymore', and 'It's Over'. Reviewers commented on his weight loss and subdued interaction with the audience. The shows were recorded for a live album that was never released, although individual cuts were used on other albums. It is possible that Parker took advantage of his client's vulnerable emotional state. An amendment made to their personal management contract at this time granted him a whopping one-third of the profits on tour dates.

The good news that the paternity suit which had long hung over his head had been dismissed by the court was short-lived. It was overshadowed by Priscilla's announcement that her reason for leaving was that she had found someone else. When Elvis returned to Los Angeles in March, it was to move out of the new home he and Priscilla had just finished remodelling.

Fortunately, Elvis had a lot to keep him occupied. Parker had put together a 15-city tour that included live recordings and a documentary. Filming of pre-tour rehearsals and recording sessions began mid-March. Elvis was pleased that these sessions included his stage band and back-up singers, rather than the usual studio musicians, but even that was not enough to lift his mood. Song choices ran to sad ballads with themes of love gone wrong: 'Separate Ways', 'For The Good Times', and 'Always On My Mind'. Finally persuaded to try something more up-tempo, he half-heartedly attempted 'Burning Love', but remained unconvinced that the song was the potential hit that others claimed. (It later reached number two in the charts.) The final session of the week ended quietly with an informal gospel sing; music that Elvis always turned to when he needed to be comforted.

Filming continued during the tour without incident. The same could not be said for the live recordings. The planned album had to be scrapped when a short in the power system fried the recording equipment on the fourth night. The finished film, *Elvis On Tour*, went on to win a 1972 Golden Globe Award for Best Documentary.

Elvis was back in Los Angeles in June to rehearse for the biggest event Parker had ever pulled off: a 14-show tour that kicked off with three shows at Madison Square Garden. Aside from his 1950s television appearances, Elvis had never before performed in New York City. He had been so savaged by the New York press on those occasions that Parker had not dared risk it. But Elvis was older now and better able to handle the pressure.

Neither Parker nor Elvis need have worried. A fourth show was hurriedly added when tickets to the original three sold out almost immediately. It sold out as well, making Elvis the first performer in history to sell out four consecutive shows at the famed venue. The *New York Times* critics were especially effusive in their praise, calling Elvis "someone in whose hands the way a thing is done becomes more important than the thing itself." The shows were recorded and the album *Elvis as Recorded Live at Madison Square Garden* was released only eight days later in order to foil bootleggers.

Soon after the tour, Elvis was introduced to 22-year-old Linda Thompson, a Memphis State College student and reigning Miss Tennessee. Although the attraction was immediate, their relationship did not develop until sometime later.

Legal separation from Priscilla came just days before Elvis began his summer Vegas shows. The divorce action was filed with the Santa Monica Superior Court three weeks later. While this was going on, Elvis sent for Linda Thompson, who remained in Las Vegas for the duration of the engagement. She would be a near-constant companion for the next few years.

The year ended with a short tour through California, culminating in three shows in Hawaii. While there, Elvis promoted the concert date he was scheduled to perform upon his return in January.

1973

Aloha From Hawaii was much more than just another concert date. As envisioned by Colonel Parker, it was a landmark media event. The $1,000,000 deal Parker put together was a first: a worldwide network television concert to be broadcast live via satellite to an estimated audience of 1.4 billion viewers. As part of the deal, RCA Records signed on to record the event for a live double album that would receive simultaneous worldwide release.

The "live" part of the promotional hype was a bit inaccurate. The show *was* broadcast live to Asia, but was shown later in the day throughout Europe. Following the show, Elvis taped five additional numbers for inclusion in the American broadcast. *Aloha From Hawaii* captured over half of the US viewing audience when it was aired in April. Elvis had lost 25 pounds for the appearance, for which he wore the now-famous jewel encrusted American Eagle jumpsuit and cape.

Elvis was back in Las Vegas two weeks later to open his eighth engagement there. The shows are plagued from the beginning with a series of cancellations due to poor health. Things got worse when four men rushed the stage during a performance and a fight ensued. Although the four turned out to be merely misguided fans, Elvis was convinced that the attack had been instigated by Priscilla's boyfriend, karate expert Mike Stone. Elvis became infuriated, accusing Stone of breaking up his marriage, and made threats to have him killed. Elvis had to be sedated several times during the tirade, but it was not until several days later that he calmed down enough to abandon the assassination plans.

In this strained emotional climate, Parker finalised the sale to RCA Records of all future rights and royalties connected to Elvis' back catalogue of recordings. The label already owned the material, but Parker had control over how it could be used, and he had consistently resisted any exploitation that might cheapen the catalogue's potential value. With Parker out of the way, the label was free to do whatever it wanted with any recording Elvis had made prior to 1973. With Elvis' agreement, a new RCA contact was signed which gave Parker a staggering 50 per cent share of all future recording income. When all of Parker's side deals were completed, he walked away with approximately $6,000,000, compared to Elvis' $4,500,000. From that point, Elvis' life began to unravel.

An eight-city tour finished out April, followed by a disastrous two weeks in Lake Tahoe, where many of the shows were cancelled due to illness. Friends and fans alike were shocked at Elvis' puffy physique and slurred speech, prompting an investigation into prescription drug abuse. Three doctors and one dentist were later identified as the main suppliers, but prosecution became impossible when Elvis refused to testify against them.

Ordered by RCA to a recording session in July, Elvis failed to show up the first night. When he did arrive the following night, studio musicians were shocked at how fat and obviously unhappy he had become since they last worked together. The sessions progressed slowly, and produced barely half of the masters the record label had specified.

Reviews of the summer Vegas shows were dismal, noting Elvis' bloated appearance and indifferent delivery. To many critics, Elvis now seemed an embarrassing caricature trying to hold on to the remnants of former glory.

Elvis' closing night shows always included gags, stunts and practical jokes. In general, the audiences loved them. This night, Colonel Parker felt that Elvis had gone too far, and told him so. Loudly. Tempers and accusations quickly escalated, fuelled by years of resentment. Elvis fired Parker, who said he would be gone as soon as Elvis paid him the share of future earnings that their contract stipulated. Parker presented a bill, which amounted to millions of dollars that Elvis did not have. The two traded insults for a week and a half before the situation returned to normal.

After renegotiating the terms of their earlier settlement, Elvis and Priscilla were granted a final divorce decree in October. The parting was amicable; they were photographed leaving the courtroom arm in arm. Within a week, Elvis was hospitalised in Memphis to find the cause of worsening breathing problems. It was finally determined that his long-standing "acupuncture" treatments had been accomplished with a daily syringe of Demerol. Elvis remained in the hospital for two weeks to detoxify from the addiction.

The year ended with sporadic recording sessions throughout the month of December. Elvis was in a much better frame of mind than when he had last recorded in July. The sessions yielded 18 masters, but the quality was no longer there.

1974

On doctor's orders, Elvis cut his winter engagement in Vegas back to two weeks. The show was generally well received by the press, who were modest in their praise. It was during this time that Elvis' habit of shooting out the screens of television sets began to be reported in the press. His temper and gun collection were a bad mix.

Parker had learned that there was big money to be made in touring, just as there had once been in films. He booked Elvis on four tours that year, besides two weeks in Lake Tahoe and the usual eight weeks in Vegas. Elvis returned to Memphis prior to his summer Vegas engagement to check on the progress at Graceland. The house was undergoing an extensive renovation under the direction of Linda Thompson. Much of what is seen at Graceland today, including the infamous "Jungle Room" dates from this period. The motive was probably less about redecorating than about keeping Linda busy: Elvis had a new girlfriend on the scene.

The August Vegas shows and the tour dates that followed drew mixed reviews, and frequently had fans wondering what it was they had witnessed. Sometimes Elvis was ill, and the shows dragged for lack of energy. Sometimes he stopped the show completely for a lengthy karate demonstration. Sometimes he launched into endless disoriented monologues about his personal life. Elvis was out of control, but the fans kept coming to watch. His life had become an impending train wreck that audiences could not turn their eyes away from.

The year ended with Elvis undergoing treatment for a stomach ulcer. A *National Enquirer* headline in November fairly well summed up the situation: "Elvis at 40 – Paunchy, Depressed and Living in Fear."

1975

Reviews of the year's Vegas shows and tour dates all reported pretty much the same thing: both Elvis and his shows had lost their magic. His weight, as well as his behaviour, had grown increasingly erratic. Another side of Elvis began to emerge, which was sometimes cruel. When the onstage insult of a female backup singer resulted in all but one of the group walking out of a performance, Elvis tried to make amends with lavish gifts of jewellery. Incidents of the sort occurred with accelerating frequency.

As usual, Elvis dealt with emotional problems by spending money. He went on a buying binge, purchasing 14 Cadillacs in a single afternoon – including one for a passing window-shopper – and spent a fortune on a fleet of private jets.

Twenty years after his first film, the opportunity for a truly meaningful acting role finally came, but at a time when Elvis was least capable of making it work. Barbra Streisand wanted him to play the male lead in *Evergreen*, her updated remake of the classic *A Star Is Born*. The offer soon got bogged down in Colonel Parker's contract demands and Elvis lost interest. Maybe he realised that his moment had passed.

The summer Vegas engagement closed after just three nights, with Elvis hospitalised for fatigue and depression. When he returned in December to make up the missed dates, the Hilton Hotel was booked solid with fans wanting to see Elvis perform. All the shows played to full houses.

1976

The profligate spending of the previous year finally caught up with Elvis. He was in severe financial straits and needed to pull himself together, but it did not appear that was likely to happen. Depressed and addicted, moody and verging on paranoia, Elvis was in trouble. His violent outbursts drove away many of those in his circle who had his best interests at heart, especially those who had urged him to seek treatment for his addiction. Those that remained often squabbled among themselves for what few spoils were left. True to form, Parker took advantage of the opportunity to introduce a new joint partnership agreement that effectively gave him half of any and all profits Elvis earned for the next seven years. For the time being, however, Parker continued to take his usual one-third share of tour profits.

Elvis needed money; he needed to tour and to record, but he was in no condition – physically or emotionally – to effectively do either. Recording sessions held at Graceland early in the year produced 'Moody Blue' and 'Hurt', which managed to place in the Top 40 on the charts, but the work was strained. Elvis showed up late, when he bothered to show up at all, and many of his key musicians had to leave before the sessions were completed in order to fulfil other commitments.

The situation did not improve when touring began in March. Fed up with Elvis' tantrums, several key members of his stage band resigned at the last minute and were hastily replaced. Elvis performed a total of 96 shows on nine separate tours that year, besides two weeks at the Sahara Tahoe Hotel in May and two weeks at the Las Vegas Hilton in December. Reviewers almost universally expressed their shock at how Elvis had deteriorated. He frequently forgot the lyrics to songs he had sung for years; he lacked energy and seemed short of breath. Elvis appeared to be sleepwalking through his performances, but the fans kept screaming. Perhaps, as one reviewer suggested, it was more for what he had once been than for what he had become. Still, the shows continued to sell out, as if fans sensed that the end was near.

The consistently poor reviews had Colonel Parker near to panic. He feared it would not be long before even hardcore Elvis fans began to desert. He even encouraged a renewed relationship between Elvis and Larry Gellar, whom Parker had banished in 1967; anything that might get his client back on track.

A recording session held at Graceland in November got off to a promising start, but quickly broke up the next night when Elvis appeared, waving a submachine gun. Unwilling to watch the continuing self-destruction, long-time girl-friend Linda Thompson decided she had had enough. She was soon replaced by Ginger Alden, a 19-year-old beauty pageant contestant Elvis had met a short time before.

1977

Elvis did not even bother to show up for the Nashville recording session planned in January. Instead, he proposed marriage to Ginger with an engagement ring containing the 10 and a half carat diamond removed from his own TCB ring.

Despite the money generated from the previous year's tours, Elvis was still in financial trouble. He continued to spend lavishly and made a series of ill-advised business invest-ments that cost him even more. Whether because of his current financial state or his planned remarriage, Elvis finally made out a will providing for his sole heir, daughter Lisa Marie Presley. Vernon was named as executor and trustee. Elvis also assigned Priscilla a deed of trust to Graceland as guarantee on the nearly half-million dollars still owed to her on the divorce settlement.

Elvis toured regularly from February through June, per-forming 55 shows. Poor health dogged him throughout the tours, with shows sometimes cut short or even cancelled. Parker rescheduled make-up dates for the end of the year, hoping that Elvis would then be in better health and spirits. While individual numbers sometimes recalled the intensity of earlier days, the overall performances were weak. Reviews were no better than they had been the previous year, with the exception that nearly every one recognised that Elvis could not go on like he was for much longer.

Still, Parker managed to pull one last deal out of his hat: a contract with CBS for a one-hour television special titled *Elvis In Concert*, to be broadcast in the fall. The footage was shot at the end of June, on Elvis' fifth and, as it turned out, final tour.

The month of July was spent in seclusion at Graceland. Lisa Marie came to visit for two weeks at the beginning of August, prior to the start of Elvis' sixth tour of the year. Elvis had some minor dental work done the day before the scheduled departure date, then retired to bed to rest until it was time to leave.

Tuesday, August 16, 1977

Elvis was found sometime around 1.30 p.m., lying in a pool of his own vomit on the floor of his bathroom. Paramedics attempted to revive him, but he was declared dead two hours later. The announcement was made that Elvis had died of cardiac arrhythmia before the autopsy had even been completed. Later lab findings confirmed that he had 14 different drugs in his system at the time of his death.

Vernon arranged a viewing at Graceland on Wednesday for the crowd of fans that had gathered outside. An estimated 50,000 people filed through the front hall and past the open copper casket. The doors were closed around 6.30 p.m. and the casket was moved into the living room for a private viewing.

A funeral service was held in the same room on Thursday afternoon. Elvis was interred early that same evening in a crypt at Forest Hill cemetery, not far from his mother's grave. The bodies of both were moved that October to their present location in the Meditation Garden behind the Graceland mansion. The CBS television special *Elvis In Concert* was broadcast the following day.

It would be easy to measure the life of Elvis Presley in statistics: the number of singles released, the number of albums sold, the number of Top 40 chart listings, the number of film roles, the number of awards. While the numbers are impressive, they only count his achievements. The real measure of Elvis' life is in the hearts he touched, the joy he brought, the emotions he stirred. By that count, the influence of his life is immeasurable.

Discography

1953: Memphis Recording Service (Sun Studio); Memphis, Tennessee

> My Happiness (Peterson/Bergantine)
> That's When Your Heartaches Begin
>   (Raskin/Brown/Fisher)

There were three objectives that drew Elvis to Memphis Recording Service in the summer of 1956: to record a gift for his mother, for Elvis to hear his own voice – a gift to himself of sorts, and to catch the attention of studio management. The first two were fulfilled. The later goal would come in time. Unable to afford duplicates, Elvis walked out of the studio with the master recording of 'My Happiness' and 'That's When Your Heartaches Begin'. Years later, he would comment that, "We still got the record at home. It's so thin that we can't play it."

January 4, 1954: Memphis Recording Service (Sun Studio); Memphis, Tennessee

> I'll Never Stand In Your Way (Hy Heath/Fred Rose)
> It Wouldn't Be The Same Without You (Jimmy
>   Wakely/Fred Rose)

Elvis returned to Memphis Recording Service to purchase two more acetate recordings in January 1954. He tried again to garner interest from Marion Keisker and Sam Phillips, leaving his name and telephone number. It will be another six months before they call. Elvis took the original recording; no copies were made.

July 5–6, 1954: Sun Studio; Memphis, Tennessee

I Love You Because (Leon Payne)
That's All Right (Arthur Crudup)
Harbor Lights (J. Kennedy/H. Williams)
Blue Moon Of Kentucky (Bill Monroe)

It was the call Elvis had been waiting for: an invitation to come record for Sam Phillips at Sun Records. Elvis made several attempts at singing 'Without You' but the song was not a good match for his voice. Still, Phillips sensed something special in him and gave his name to guitarist Scott Moore – half of the duo, The Starlight Wranglers – and suggested he call the young singer. Moore did. He and bassist Bill Black rehearsed with Elvis, and later Phillips made another attempt at capturing Elvis' voice. They recorded four songs, of which 'That's All Right' with flipside 'Blue Moon of Kentucky' became Elvis' first single. It sold over 6,300 copies in the Memphis area alone. Elvis, who was still underage, had his parents sign a contract with Scotty to act as manager and booking agent, and with Sam Phillips to record for Sun Records.

August 19, 1954: Sun Studio; Memphis, Tennessee

Blue Moon (Rodgers/Hart)

Sept 10, 1954: Sun Studio; Memphis, Tennessee

Tomorrow Night (Sam Coslow/Will Grosz)
Satisfied (Martha Carson)
I'll Never Let You Go (Little Darlin') (Jimmy Wakely)
I Don't Care If The Sun Don't Shine (Mack David)
Just Because (Bob & Joe Shelton/Sid Robin)
Good Rockin' Tonight (Roy Brown)

Elvis' second single, 'Good Rockin' Tonight'/'I Don't Care If The Sun Don't Shine', was released in September 1954.

October 16, 1954: Live Recordings for "The Louisiana Hayride", Municipal Auditorium; Shreveport, Louisiana

That's All Right (Arthur Crudup)
Blue Moon Of Kentucky (Bill Monroe)

December 1954: Studio Sessions, Sun Studio; Memphis, Tennessee

Milkcow Blues Boogie (Kokomo Arnold)
You're A Heartbreaker (Jack Sallee)

'Milkcow Blues Boogie'/'You're A Heartbreaker' was Elvis' third single. A review in the January 19, 1955 issue of *Billboard* magazine said that Elvis "continues to impress".

Jan or Feb 1955: Radio Recording; Lubbock, Texas

Fool, Fool, Fool (Nugetre)
Shake, Rattle And Roll (Charles Calhoun)

February 1955: Studio Sessions, Sun Studio; Memphis, Tennessee

I Got A Woman (Ray Charles)
Trying To Get To You (McCoy/Singleton)
Baby Let's Play House (Arthur Gunter)

March 1955: Studio Sessions, Sun Studio; Memphis, Tennessee

I'm Left, You're Right, She's Gone (slow version)
    (Kesler/Taylor)
I'm Left, You're Right, She's Gone (Kesler/Taylor)

March 19, 1955: Live Recordings, Eagles Hall; Houston, Texas

> Good Rockin' Tonight (Roy Brown)
> Baby Let's Play House (Arthur Gunter)
> Blue Moon Of Kentucky (Bill Monroe)
> I Got A Woman (Ray Charles)
> That's All Right (Arthur Crudup)

Elvis' fourth single, 'Baby Let's Play House', with B-side 'I'm Left, You're Right, She's Gone' was released April 1955. The song was met with controversy over the suggestive lyrics.

April 30, 1955: Live Recordings; Gladewater, Texas

> Tweedle Dee (Winfield Scott)

July 11, 1955: Studio Sessions, Sun Studio; Memphis, Tennessee

> I Forgot To Remember To Forget (Stan Kesler/Charles Feathers)
> Mystery Train (Junior Parker/Sam Phillips)
> Trying To Get To You (Singleton/McCoy)

August 1955, Sun Records released 'I Forgot To Remember To Forget'/'Mystery Train', Elvis' fifth and final single for the label.

November 1955: Studio Sessions, Sun Studio; Memphis, Tennessee

> When It Rains, It Really Pours (William Emerson)

Colonel Parker signed Elvis to a management contract. He then struck a deal for RCA to purchase Elvis' recording contract from Sun Records for $35,000. On 2 December 1955, RCA re-released Sun singles 'I Forgot To Remember To Forget'/

'Mystery Train' and on 20 December, also re-released the first four singles. February 1956, 'I Forgot To Remember To Forget' reached the top of *Billboard*'s country-and-western chart.

January 10–11, 1956: Studio Sessions for RCA, RCA Studios; Nashville, Tennessee

I Got A Woman (Ray Charles)
Heartbreak Hotel (Mae Boren Axton/Tommy
    Durden/Elvis Presley)
Money Honey (Jesse Stone)
I'm Counting On You (Don Robertson)
I Was The One (Schroeder/DeMetrius/Blair/Peppers)

In January 1956, Elvis began recording for RCA. The first session was disastrous. Label executives grumbled that the signing was a big mistake and had no faith in the first release, 'Heartbreak Hotel'/'I Was The One'. But Elvis fans loved the record and rushed to stores to buy a copy. 'Heartbreak Hotel' became Elvis' first number one hit and it remained at the top of the charts for seven weeks. By April, the record had sold over a million copies and became *Billboard*'s number one single for 1956. All six of Elvis' singles hit RCA's top 25 best-sellers chart in March. Later that month, RCA released Elvis' first album, titled simply *Elvis Presley*. The LP sold over 300,000 copies in its initial chart run, taking it to number one for 10 weeks, and became RCA's biggest selling pop album to date.

January 30–31 and February 3, 1956: Studio Sessions for RCA, RCA Studios; New York, New York

Blue Suede Shoes (Carl Perkins)
My Baby Left Me (Arthur Crudup)
One-Sided Love Affair (Bill Campbell)

So Glad You're Mine (Arthur Crudup)
I'm Gonna Sit Right Down and Cry (Over You)
(Thomas/Biggs)
Tutti Frutti (Dorothy LaBostrie/Richard Penniman)
Lawdy, Miss Clawdy (Lloyd Price)
Shake, Rattle And Roll (Charles Calhoun)

January–March 1956: TV Soundtrack Recordings for CBS's *Stage Show*, CBS Studios; New York, New York

January 28

Shake, Rattle And Roll/Flip, Flop and Fly (Charles
Calhoun; Charles Calhoun/Lou Willie Turner)
I Got A Woman (Ray Charles)

February 4

Baby Let's Play House (Arthur Gunter)
Tutti Frutti (Dorothy LaBostrie/Richard Penniman)

February 11

Blue Suede Shoes (Carl Perkins)
Heartbreak Hotel (Axton/Durden/Presley)

February 18

Tutti Frutti (Dorothy LaBostrie/Richard Penniman)
I Was The One (Schroeder/DeMetrius/Blair/Peppers)

March 17

Blue Suede Shoes (Carl Perkins)
Heartbreak Hotel (Axton/Durden/Presley)

March 24

Money Honey (Jesse Stone)
Heartbreak Hotel (Axton/Durden/Presley)

April 3, 1956: TV Soundtrack Recordings for NBC's *The Milton Berle Show*

The U.S.S. Hancock; San Diego Naval Station, California
Shake, Rattle And Roll (Charles Calhoun)
Heartbreak Hotel (Axton/Durden/Presley)
Blue Suede Shoes (Carl Perkins)

Elvis made his television debut April 3, 1956, on "The Milton Berle Show", broadcast from the deck of The USS Hancock aircraft carrier. He performed 'Blue Suede Shoes', 'Heartbreak Hotel', and 'Shake, Rattle and Roll', and was paid $3,000 for his appearance.

April 14, 1956: Studio Sessions for RCA, RCA Studios; Nashville, Tennessee

I Want You, I Need You, I Love You (Maurice Mysels/Ira Kosloff)

May 6, 1956: Private Recordings, Venus Room, New Frontier Hotel; Las Vegas, Nevada

Heartbreak Hotel (Axton/Durden/Presley)
Long Tall Sally (Johnson/Penniman/Blackwell)
Blue Suede Shoes (Carl Perkins)
Money Honey (Jesse Stone)

June 5, 1956: TV Soundtrack Recordings for NBC's *The Milton Berle Show*, NBC Studios; Los Angeles, California

Hound Dog (Jerry Leiber/Mike Stoller)
I Want You, I Need You, I Love You (Maurice Mysels/Ira Kosloff)

During his June 5, 1956 appearance on "The Milton Berle Show", Elvis was presented with a *Billboard* award for scoring number one on the retail, disc jockey and jukebox charts for both pop and country-and-western for 'Heartbreak Hotel'. He performed the hit, along with 'I Want You, I Need You, I Love You' and 'Hound Dog'. His hip-swivelling rendition of the later song caused an uproar. Critic John Crosby of the *New York Herald Tribune* wrote Elvis was "unspeakably untalented and vulgar". Others called the performance "obscene" and nothing more than "sexual self-gratification onstage", but the bad press did nothing to diminish Elvis' popularity.

July 1, 1956: TV Soundtrack Recordings for NBC's *Steve Allen Show*, The Hudson Theatre; New York, New York

I Want You, I Need You, I Love You (Maurice Mysels/Ira Kosloff)
Hound Dog (Jerry Leiber/Mike Stoller)

July 2, 1956: Studio Sessions for RCA, RCA Studios, New York, NY

Hound Dog (Jerry Leiber/Mike Stoller)
Don't Be Cruel (Otis Blackwell/Elvis Presley)
Any Way You Want Me (Aaron Schroeder/Cliff Owens)

July 1956, RCA released 'Don't Be Cruel'/'Hound Dog' and soon found they had massive selling double-hits on their hands. 'Hound Dog' rocketed to the number two slot and sold over one million copies, then 'Don't Be Cruel' soared to number one on *Billboard*'s Top 100, taking sales on the double-sided hit to nearly four million copies. In August, RCA released six singles simultaneously, an industry first: 'Blue Suede Shoes'/ 'Tutti Frutti', 'I Got A Woman'/'I'm Counting On You', 'I'll

Never Let You Go'/'I'm Gonna Sit Right Down And Cry', 'I Love You Because'/'Trying To Get To You', 'Just Because'/ 'Blue Moon', 'Money Honey'/'One-Sided Love Affair', 'Shake, Rattle and Roll'/'Lawdy, Miss Clawdy'.

August 24, September 4–5, October 1, 1956: Soundtrack Recordings for 20th Century Fox's *Love Me Tender*

Fox Stage 1; Hollywood, California

August 24

We're Gonna Move (Vera Matson/Elvis Presley)
Love Me Tender (Vera Matson/Elvis Presley)
Poor Boy (Vera Matson/Elvis Presley)

September 4

Let Me (Vera Matson/Elvis Presley)

October 1

Love Me Tender (end title version) (Vera Matson/ Elvis Presley)

At the beginning of April 1956, Elvis' dream of being an actor was about to come true. He flew to Hollywood and to screen test with Hal Wallis of Paramount Pictures. Days later, Wallis signed Elvis to a three picture deal. When no suitable vehicle was found for Elvis, he was loaned out to Twentieth Century Fox to make his film debut in *Love Me Tender*. Principle photography for the film, which was originally titled *The Reno Brothers*, began August 22, 1956, with recording for the sound-track starting the following day. After his regular band members Scotty Moore, Bill Black and JD Fontana were rejected by the film's musical director, Elvis was forced to record the *Love Me Tender* soundtrack with unfamiliar studio musicians. The ballad 'Love Me Tender' was a departure from the upbeat tunes Elvis had been recording and struck a chord with the singer. "I used

155

to sing nothing but ballads before I went professional," he told reporter Army Archend. "I love ballads." The film's title was changed to *Love Me Tender* and the single, 'Love Me Tender'/ 'Any Way You Want Me' hit number one on *Billboard*'s Top 100. By year's end, it had sold over 2.5 million copies.

September 1–3, 1956: Studio Sessions for RCA, Radio Recorders; Hollywood, California

September 1

Playing For Keeps (Stanley A. Kesler)
Love Me (Jerry Leiber/Mike Stoller)
How Do You Think I Feel (Walker/Pierce)
How's The World Treating You (Chet
 Atkins/Boudleaux Bryant)

September 2

When My Blue Moon Turns To Gold Again (Wiley
 Walker/Gene Sullivan)
Long Tall Sally (Enotris Johnson)
Old Shep (Red Foley)
Paralyzed (Otis Blackwell/Elvis Presley)
Too Much (Lee Rosenberg/Leonard Weinman)
Anyplace Is Paradise (Joe Thomas)

September 3

Ready Teddy (Blackwell/Marascalco)
First In Line (Aaron Schroeder/Ben Weisman)
Rip It Up (Robert Blackwell/John Marascalco)

September 9, 1956: TV Recordings for CBS's *Toast Of The Town*, CBS Studios; Los Angeles, California

Don't Be Cruel (Otis Blackwell/Elvis Presley)
Love Me Tender (Vera Matson/Elvis Presley)

Ready Teddy (Blackwell/Marascalco)
Hound Dog (Jerry Leiber/Mike Stoller)

September 26, 1956: Private Recordings, Mississippi–Alabama Fair and Dairy Show; Tupelo, Mississippi

Afternoon Show

Heartbreak Hotel (Axton/Durden/Presley)
Long Tall Sally (Enotris Johnson)
I Was The One (Schroeder/DeMetrius/Blair/Peppers)
I Want You, I Need You, I Love You (Maurice Mysels/Ira Kosloff)
I Got A Woman (Ray Charles)
Don't Be Cruel (Otis Blackwell/Elvis Presley)
Ready Teddy (Blackwell/Marascalco)
Love Me Tender (Vera Matson/Elvis Presley)
Hound Dog (Jerry Leiber/Mike Stoller)

Evening Show

Love Me Tender (Vera Matson/Elvis Presley)
I Was The One (Schroeder/DeMetrius/Blair/Peppers)
I Got A Woman (Ray Charles)
Don't Be Cruel (Otis Blackwell/Elvis Presley)
Blue Suede Shoes (Carl Perkins)
Baby Let's Play House (Arthur Gunter)
Hound Dog (Jerry Leiber/Mike Stoller)

October 28, 1956: TV Recordings for CBS's *Toast Of The Town*, CBS Studios; New York, New York

Don't Be Cruel (Otis Blackwell/Elvis Presley)
Love Me Tender (Vera Matson/Elvis Presley)
Love Me (Jerry Leiber/Mike Stoller)
Hound Dog (Jerry Leiber/Mike Stoller)

RCA had advance orders of one million for the single 'Love Me Tender'/'Any Way You Want Me', earning Elvis his fifth gold record in 1956. The single entered *Billboard*'s Top 100 chart at number nine and moved up to number one by November 7. The film *Love Me Tender* opened in theatres November 15 and was a hit.

December 4, 1956: Jam Session, Sun Studios; Memphis, Tennessee

You Belong To My Heart (Ray Gilbert/Augustin Lara)
When God Dips His Love In My Heart (Traditional)
Just A Little Talk With Jesus (Clevant Derricks)
Jesus Walked That Lonesome Valley (Traditional)
I Shall Not Be Moved (Traditional)
(There'll Be) Peace In The Valley (For Me)
    (Thomas A. Dorsey)
Down By The Riverside (Traditional)
I'm With A Crowd But So Alone (Ernest Tubb/
    Carl Story)
Farther Along (Traditional)
Blessed Jesus (Hold My Hand) (Traditional)
On The Jericho Road (Traditional)
I Just Can't Make It By Myself (Herbert Brewster)
Little Cabin On The Hill (Bill Monroe/Lester Flatt)
Summertime Is Past And Gone (Bill Monroe)
I Hear A Sweet Voice Calling (Bill Monroe)
Sweetheart You Done Me Wrong (Bill Monroe)
Keeper Of The Key (Beverly Stewart/Harlan
    Howard/Kenny Devine/Lance Guynes)
Crazy Arms (Ralph Mooney/Charlie Seals)
Don't Forbid Me (Charles Singleton)
Too Much Monkey Business (Chuck Berry)
Brown Eyed Handsome Man (Chuck Berry)

Out Of Sight, Out Of Mind (Ivory Joe Hunter/
    Clyde Otis)
Brown Eyed Handsome Man (Chuck Berry)
Reconsider Baby (Lowell Fulsom)
Don't Be Cruel (Otis Blackwell/Elvis Presley)
Don't Be Cruel (Otis Blackwell/Elvis Presley)
Paralyzed (Otis Blackwell/Elvis Presley)
Don't Be Cruel (Otis Blackwell/Elvis Presley)
There's No Place Like Home (John Howard
    Payne/Henry Rowley Bishop)
When The Saints Go Marching In (Traditional)
Softly And Tenderly (Traditional)
Is It So Strange (Faron Young)
That's When Your Heartaches Begin
    (Hill/Fisher/Raskin)
Brown Eyed Handsome Man (Chuck Berry)
Rip It Up (Robert Blackwell/John Marascalco)
I'm Gonna Bid My Blues Goodbye (Hank Snow)

December 1956: Private Recordings, Audubon Drive; Memphis, Tennessee

When The Saints Go Marching In (Traditional)

January 6, 1957: TV Soundtrack Recordings for CBS's *Toast Of The Town*, CBS Studios; New York, New York

Hound Dog (Jerry Leiber/Mike Stoller)
Love Me Tender (Vera Matson/Elvis Presley)
Heartbreak Hotel (Axton/Durden/Presley)
Don't Be Cruel (Otis Blackwell/Elvis Presley)
Too Much (Lee Rosenberg/Bernard Weinman)
When My Blue Moon Turns To Gold Again
    (Wiley Walker/Gene Sullivan)

(There'll Be) Peace In The Valley (For Me) (Thomas
A. Dorsey)

'Too Much', with flipside, 'Playing For Keep', was released in
January 1957. The single only made it to number two on the
charts, but sold two million copies. Elvis began recording the
soundtrack for *Loving You* on January15 and the film started
shooting on the 21st.

January 12–13, 1957: Studio Sessions for RCA, Radio Recorders; Hollywood, California

January 12

I Believe (Drake/Graham/Shirl/Stillman)
Tell Me Why (Titus Turner)
Got A Lot O' Livin' To Do (Aaron Schroeder/
Ben Weisman)
All Shook Up (Otis Blackwell/E. Presley)

January 13

Mean Woman Blues (Claude DeMetrius)
(There'll Be) Peace In The Valley (For Me)
(Thomas A. Dorsey)
I Beg Of You (Rosemarie McCoy/Kelly Owens)
That's When Your Heartaches Begin
(Raskin/Brown/Fisher)
Take My Hand, Precious Lord (Thomas A. Dorsey)

January 15–18: Soundtrack Recordings for Paramount's *Loving You*, Paramount Scoring Stage; Hollywood, California

(Let's Have A) Party (vocal and band) (Jessie Mae
Robinson)
Lonesome Cowboy (Sid Tepper/Roy C. Bennett)

Got A Lot O' Livin' To Do (opening) (Aaron
Schroeder/Ben Weisman)
(Let Me Be Your) Teddy Bear (Kal Mann/Bernie Lowe)
Loving You (end version) (Jerry Leiber/Mike Stoller)
Loving You (main version) (Jerry Leiber/Mike Stoller)
One Night (Of Sin) (Bartholomew/King)
Blueberry Hill (A. Lewis/L. Stock/V. Rose)
Hot Dog (Jerry Leiber/Mike Stoller)
Got A Lot O' Livin' To Do (finale) (Aaron
Schroeder/Ben Weisman)

January 19, 1957: Studio Sessions for RCA, Radio Recorders; Hollywood, California

It Is No Secret (What God Can Do) (Stuart Hamblen)
Blueberry Hill (A. Lewis/L. Stock/V. Rose)
Have I Told You Lately That I Love You (Scott
Wiseman)
Is It So Strange (Faron Young)

January 21–22: Soundtrack Recordings for Paramount's *Loving You*, Paramount Scoring Stage; Hollywood, California

(Let's Have A) Party (vocal and group) (Jessie Mae
Robinson)
Mean Woman Blues (Claude DeMetrius)
Loving You (farm version) (Jerry Leiber/Mike Stoller)

February 14, 1957: Soundtrack Recordings for Paramount's *Loving You*, Radio Recorders; Hollywood, California

Loving You (main version) (Jerry Leiber/Mike Stoller)
Loving You (farm version) (Jerry Leiber/Mike Stoller)

February 23–24, 1957: Studio Sessions for RCA, Radio Recorders; Hollywood, California

February 23

Don't Leave Me Now (Aaron Schroeder/Ben
    Weisman)
I Beg Of You (Rose Marie McCoy/Kelly Owens)
One Night (Bartholomew/King)
True Love (Cole Porter)
I Need You So (Ivory Joe Hunter)

February 24

Loving You (Jerry Leiber/Mike Stoller)
When It Rains, It Really Pours (William Robert
    Emerson)

Released in March 1957, 'All Shook Up' with B-side 'That's When Your Heartaches Begin' reached number one on *Billboard*'s Top 100, remained there for eight weeks, and sold just short of 2.5 million copies.

April 30, 1957: Soundtrack Recordings for MGM's *Jailhouse Rock*, Radio Recorders; Hollywood, California

Jailhouse Rock (Jerry Leiber/Mike Stoller)
Jailhouse Rock (movie version) (Jerry Leiber/
    Mike Stoller)
Young And Beautiful (movie end) (Abner Silver/
    Aaron Schroeder)
Young And Beautiful (Abner Silver/Aaron Schroeder)
Young And Beautiful (jail version) (Abner Silver/
    Aaron Schroeder)
Young And Beautiful (Florida Club version)
    (Abner Silver/Aaron Schroeder)

May 3, 1957: Soundtrack Recordings for MGM's *Jailhouse Rock*, Radio Recorders; Hollywood, California

Treat Me Nice (Jerry Leiber/Mike Stoller)

I Want To Be Free (jail version) (Jerry Leiber/
     Mike Stoller)

I Want To Be Free ((Jerry Leiber/Mike Stoller)

(You're So Square) Baby I Don't Care (Jerry Leiber/
     Mike Stoller)

Don't Leave Me Now (movie version – not used)
     (Aaron Schroeder/Ben Weisman)

Don't Leave Me Now (Aaron Schroeder/
     Ben Weisman)

May 9, 1957: Soundtrack Recordings for MGM's *Jailhouse Rock*, MGM Soundstage; Hollywood, California

Don't Leave Me Now (Aaron Schroeder/
     Ben Weisman)

Don't Leave Me Now (Aaron Schroeder/
     Ben Weisman)

In June 1957, 'Teddy Bear'/'Loving You' was released, went to number one, and sold over a million copies. It was Elvis' first single to be released in the UK.

Elvis began recording the soundtrack for *Jailhouse Rock* at the end of April and filming for the movie on May 13. It premiered in Memphis on October 17 and opened across the country three weeks later. Fans loved that Elvis sang and performed in big dance numbers for the film. Choreographer Alex Romero watched and worked with Elvis to mimic his unique style – the result captured the unadulterated energy and enthusiasm of his live shows. The first singles from the film, 'Jailhouse Rock' with B-side 'Treat Me Nice' was a number one hit and sold over three million copies in the US within the next 12 months. It was Elvis' first single to reach number one in the UK charts.

September 5–7, 1957: Studio Sessions for RCA, Radio Recorders; Hollywood, California

September 5

Treat Me Nice (Jerry Leiber/Mike Stoller)
Blue Christmas (Billy Hayes/Jay Johnston)

September 6

My Wish Came True (Ivory Joe Hunter)
White Christmas (Irving Berlin)
Here Comes Santa Claus (Gene Autry/
    Oakley Haldeman)
Silent Night (Joseph Mohr/Franz Gruber)
Don't (Jerry Leiber/Mike Stoller)

September 7

O Little Town Of Bethlehem (Philips Brooks/
    Lewis Redner)
Santa Bring My Baby Back (To Me) (Aaron
    Schroeder/Claude DeMetrius)
Santa Claus Is Back In Town (Jerry Leiber/
    Mike Stoller)
I'll Be Home For Christmas (Gannon/Kent/Ram)

January 15–16 and 23, 1958: Soundtrack Recordings for Paramount's *King Creole*, Radio Recorders; Hollywood, California

January 15

Hard Headed Woman (Claude DeMetrius)
Trouble (Jerry Leiber/Mike Stoller)
New Orleans (Sid Tepper/Roy C. Bennett)

King Creole (Jerry Leiber/Mike Stoller)
Crawfish (Fred Wise/Ben Weisman)

January 16

Dixieland Rock (Claude DeMetrius/Fred Wise)
Lover Doll (Sid Wayne/Abner Silver)
Don't Ask Me Why (Fred Wise/Ben Weisman)
As Long As I Have You (Fred Wise/Ben Weisman)
Steadfast, Loyal and True (movie version) (Jerry Leiber/
    Mike Stoller)
As Long As I Have You (movie version) (Fred Wise/
    Ben Weisman)

January 23

King Creole (Jerry Leiber/Mike Stoller)
Young Dreams (Martin Kalmanoff/Aaron Schroeder)

Elvis' kicked off 1958 with the release of the single 'Don't'/
'I Beg Of You' which rocketed to number one and sold
1.3 million. The song was written for Elvis by Jerry Leiber and
Mike Stoller. Later in the month, Elvis began recording songs
for his next picture, *King Creole* with Leiber and Stoller, who
later go on to reach superstar status as songwriters. In February,
Elvis continued work on the soundtrack, while also trying to
create a backlog of songs to be released while he was away
serving in the army.

February 1, 1958: Studio Sessions for RCA, Radio Recorders; Hollywood, California

My Wish Came True (Ivory Joe Hunter)
Doncha' Think It's Time (Clyde Otis/Willie Dixon)
Your Cheatin' Heart (Hank Williams)
Wear My Ring Around Your Neck (Burt Carroll/
    Russell Moody)

February 11, 1958: Soundtrack Recordings for Paramount's *King Creole*, Paramount Soundstage; Hollywood, California

Danny (Fred Wise/Ben Weisman)
Steadfast, Loyal and True (Jerry Leiber/Mike Stoller)

In April, 'Wear My Ring' with B-side 'Doncha' Think It's Time' was released. While the A-side climbed to number three and the flip side to number 21, the record sold considerably less than previous releases, which further exacerbated Colonel Parker and RCA executives' concerns that Elvis' popularity might diminish while he was serving in the military. Anxiety intensified when the June-released single 'Hard Headed Woman'/'Don't Ask Me Why' from the *King Creole* soundtrack went to number two, but sold just one million copies – about half what was expected a year earlier.

June 10, 1958: Studio Sessions for RCA, RCA's Studio B; Nashville, Tennessee

I Need Your Love Tonight (Sid Wayne/Bix Reichner)
A Big Hunk O' Love (Aaron Schroeder/Sid Wayne)
Ain't That Loving You Baby (Clyde Otis/Ivory Joe Hunter)
(Now And Then There's) A Fool Such As I (Bill Trader)
I Got Stung (Aaron Schroeder/David Hill)

While serving in the army, Elvis was awarded his first RIAA Gold Disc for 'Hard Headed Woman' on August 11, 1958.

Elvis had reservations about releasing a soundtrack album for *King Creole*. He felt there was not enough good material to merit an album. But to cash in on the publicity surrounding Elvis' entering military service, an album was pulled together and released in September. It rose to number two on the charts and sold 250,000 copies, in spite of the fact that all but one track had previously been released as a single or EP. In October, 'One Night'/'I Got Stung' was released, a year after it had been recorded. Elvis doubted the song was strong enough to be a single, but finally acquiesced to its release. The A-side climbed to number four and the B-side to number eight, selling 1.5 million and making it Elvis' best selling single since 'Jailhouse Rock'.

In a continuing effort to hold onto Elvis' popularity while he was stationed in Germany, RCA released the single 'A Fool Such As I' with B-side 'I Need Your Love Tonight' in March 1959, from the June 1958 recording sessions. Fans ate it up, purchasing over a million copies and propelling the A-side to number two and the B-Side to number four. It was only the second time both sides had reached the Top 5. The first was 'Hound Dog' with 'Don't Be Cruel'. The June release of 'A Big Hunk O' Love'/'My Wish Came True' earned Elvis another number one single and sales of one million copies. It was the last single released before Elvis was discharged from the army, nearly nine months later. The LP *A Date With Elvis* was shipped in July. The album was made up of previously released cuts, including the five Sun singles and the film soundtrack singles. Colonel Parker convinced RCA to include a calendar that counted down the days until Elvis' release from the army, along with photographs of G.I. Elvis.

April 1959: Home Recordings, Goethestrasse; Bad Nauheim, Germany

> I'm Beginning To Forget You (Phelps)
> I Can't Help It (If I'm Still In Love With You)
>   (Hank Williams)
> Mona Lisa (Livingston/Evans;
> Danny Boy (Weatherly)
> Loving You (Jerry Leiber/Mike Stoller)
> I'm Beginning To Forget You (a capella) (Phelps)

April 1959 (or Later): Home Recordings, Goethestrasse; Bad Nauheim, Germany

He Knows Just What I Need (Mosie Lister)
Cool Water (Bob Nolan)
His Hand In Mine (Mosie Lister)
Return To Me (Carmen Lombardo/Danny Di Minno)
Are You Lonesome Tonight? (Roy Turk/
    Lou Handman)
Stand By You (Traditional)
Take My Hand, Precious Lord (Thomas A. Dorsey)
Oh, Lonesome Me (Don Gibson)

After April 1959: Home Recordings, Goethestrasse; Bad Nauheim, Germany

I Asked The Lord (Johnny Lange/Jimmy Duncan)
Apron Strings (Weiss/Schroeder)
Soldier Boy (Jones/Williams Jr)
Earth Angel (Belvin)
I'll Take You Home Again Kathleen (fast version)
    (Thomas P. Westendorf)
Que Sera, Sera/Hound Dog (Jay Livingston/Ray
    Evans; Jerry Leiber/Mike Stoller)
I'll Take You Home Again Kathleen (Traditional)
It's Been So Long Darling (Ernest Tubb)
I Will Be True (Ivory Joe Hunter)
There's No Tomorrow (Hoffman/Corday/Carr)
Unidentified (possibly called 'Number Eight')
Send Me Some Lovin' (Marascalco/Price)
The Fool (Naomi Ford)

Elvis rented a piano and began working up songs and recording them on a home tape recorder. Many of the songs were gospel hymns – a genre Elvis had loved since he was a young boy – that would later be re-recorded and released on the 1960s album *His Hand In Mine*.

Throughout the end of 1958 until spring 1960, RCA continued to release albums and EP's from Elvis' catalogue.

March 20, 1960: Studio Sessions for RCA, RCA's Studio B; Nashville, Tennessee

Make Me Know It (Otis Blackwell)
Soldier Boy (David Jones/Theodore Williams Jr)
Stuck On You (Aaron Schroeder/S. Leslie McFarland)
Fame And Fortune (Fred Wise/Ben Weisman)
A Mess Of Blues (Doc Pomus/Mort Shuman)
It Feels So Right (Fred Wise/Ben Weisman)

In order to keep the press and fans away from the first recording session since Elvis' release from the military, musicians were told they were being booked for a Jim Reeves session. The session began at 8.00 p.m. and continued through the night, finishing up six sides by 7.00 a.m. 'Stuck On You'/'Fame And Fortune' was released just days later. RCA shipped one million copies of the single, which rose to number one and remained there for three weeks. In April, the aptly titled LP *Elvis Is Back* hit stores and leaped to number two. While it was critically well-received, it sold less than 300,000 copies.

March 26, 1960: TV Recordings for ABC's *The Frank Sinatra Timex Show*, Fontainebleau Hotel; Miami, Florida

It's Nice To Go Trav'ling (Sammy Cahn/Jimmy Van Heusen)
Fame And Fortune (Fred Wise/Ben Weisman)
Stuck On You (Aaron Schroeder/S. Leslie McFarland)
Witchcraft/Love Me Tender (C. Coleman/C. Leigh; V. Matson/E. Presley)

April 3, 1960: Studio Sessions for RCA, RCA's Studio B; Nashville, Tennessee

Fever (John Davenport/Eddie Cooley)
Like A Baby (Jesse Stone)
It's Now Or Never (Aaron Schroeder/Wally Gold)
The Girl Of My Best Friend (Beverly Rose/
    Sam Bobrick)
Dirty, Dirty Feeling (Jerry Leiber/Mike Stoller)
Thrill Of Your Love (Stanley Kesler)
I Gotta Know (P. Evans/M. Williams)
Such A Night (Lincoln Chase)
Are You Lonesome Tonight? (Roy Turk/
    Lou Handman)
The Girl Next Door Went A'Walking (Bill
    Rise/Thomas Wayne)
I Will Be Home Again (Benjamin/Leveen/Singer)
Reconsider Baby (Lowell Fulson)

Released in April, 'It's Now Or Never'/'A Mess Of Blues' went to number one in the US and UK charts, and earned over \$4.5 million in sales worldwide, becoming Elvis' biggest hit. It was named *Billboard*'s Vocal Single of the Year for 1960.

April 27–28, 1960: Soundtrack Recordings for Paramount's *G. I. Blues*, RCA Studios; Hollywood, California

Shoppin' Around (Tepper/Bennett/Schroeder)
Didja' Ever (Sid Wayne/Sherman Edwards)
Doin' The Best I Can (Doc Pomus/Mort Shuman)
G. I. Blues (Sid Tepper/Roy C. Bennett)
Frankfort Special (Sid Wayne/Sherman Edwards)
Tonight Is So Right For Love (Sid Wayne/
    Abner Silver)

Big Boots (Sid Wayne/Sherman Edwards)
Big Boots (slow) (Sid Wayne/Sherman Edwards)
What's She Really Like (Sid Wayne/Sherman Edwards)
Blue Suede Shoes (Carl Perkins)
Wooden Heart (Wise/Weisman/Twomey)
Pocketful Of Rainbows (Fred Wise/Ben Weisman)

May 6, 1960: Sound track Recordings for Paramount's *G. I. Blues*, Radio Recorders; Hollywood, California

Big Boots (fast) (Sid Wayne/Sherman Edwards)
Shoppin' Around (Tepper/Bennett/Schroeder)
Pocketful Of Rainbows (Fred Wise/Ben Weisman)
Frankfort Special (Sid Wayne/Sherman Edwards)
Tonight's All Right For Love (Wayne/Silver/
    Joe Willey)
Big Boots (Sid Wayne/Sherman Edwards)
Big Boots (insert) (Sid Wayne/Sherman Edwards)
Big Boots (composite) (Sid Wayne/Sherman Edwards)

August 8, 1960: Soundtrack Recordings for 20th Century-Fox's *Flaming Star*, Radio Recorders; Hollywood, California

Black Star (Sid Wayne/Sherman Edwards)
Black Star (end title) (Sid Wayne/Sherman Edwards)
Summer Kisses, Winter Tears (Wise/Weisman/Lloyd)
Britches (Sid Wayne/Sherman Edwards)
A Cane And A High Starched Collar (Sid Tepper/
    Roy C. Bennett)
Summer Kisses, Winter Tears (movie version)
    (Wise/Weisman/Lloyd)

171

October 7, 1960: Soundtrack Recordings for 20th Century-Fox's *Flaming Star*, Radio Recorders; Hollywood, California

Flaming Star (Sid Wayne/Sherman Edwards)
Flaming Star (end title) (Sid Wayne/
Sherman Edwards)

October 30, 1960: Studio Sessions for RCA, RCA's Studio B; Nashville, Tennessee

Milky White Way (arranged and adapted by Elvis
Presley)
His Hand In Mine (Mosie Lister)
I Believe In The Man In The Sky
(Richard Howard)
He Knows Just What I Need (Mosie Lister)
Surrender (Doc Pomus/Mort Shuman)
Mansion Over The Hilltop (Ira Stamphill)
In My Father's House (Allecne Hanks)
Joshua Fit The Battle (arranged and adapted by
Elvis Presley)
Swing Down Sweet Chariot (arranged and adapted by
Elvis Presley)
I'm Gonna Walk Dem Golden Stairs (Cully Holt)
If We Never Meet Again (Albert E. Brumley)
Known Only To Him (Stuart Hamblen)
Crying In The Chapel (Artie Glenn)
Working On The Building (W. O. Hoyle/
Lillian Bowles)

Though Elvis was not crazy about the material for the film and soundtrack to *G.I. Blues,* the October-released album sold over 700,000 units, setting a new sales record that surpassed the success of *Elvis Is Back.*

November 7–8, 1960: Soundtrack Sessions for 20th Century-Fox's *Wild In The Country*, Radio Recorders; Hollywood, California

Lonely Man (Bennie Benjamin/Sol Marcus)
Lonely Man (solo) (Bennie Benjamin/Sol Marcus)
In My Way (Fred Wise/Ben Weisman)
Wild In The Country (Peretti/Creatore/Weiss)
Forget Me Never (Fred Wise/Ben Weisman)
I Slipped, I Stumbled, I Fell (Fred Wise/Ben Weisman)
I Slipped, I Stumbled, I Fell (lower key) (Fred Wise/
     Ben Weisman)

Fall 1960: Private Recordings, Monovale Drive; Hollywood, California

You'll Never Walk Alone (Rodgers/Hammerstein)
If I Loved You (Rodgers/Hammerstein)
The Lord's Prayer (Traditional)
I Wonder, I Wonder, I Wonder (Daryl Hutchinson)
An Evening Prayer (incomplete) (Battersby/Gabriel)
Make Believe (Hammerstein/Kern)
She Wears My Ring (Boudleaux Bryant/Felice Bryant)
Sweet Leilani (Harry Owens)
Beyond The Reef (incomplete) (Pitman)
When The Swallows Come Back To Capistrano
     (Leon Rene)
He (J. Richards/R. Mullen)
Hands Off (Bowman/McShann)
Lawdy Miss Clawdy (incomplete) (Lloyd Price)

'Are You Lonesome Tonight?'/'I Gotta Know' was shipped in November. It sold over two million copies and was another number one hit. More importantly to Elvis, so was the release of his gospel LP *His Hand In Mine* the same month. It was the culmination of a dream to pay tribute to the music he grew up with and had always loved. It was also a tribute to his mother and the faith she instilled in him from an early age.

March 12, 1961: Studio Sessions for RCA, RCA's Studio B; Nashville, Tennessee

I'm Comin' Home (Charlie Rich)
Gentry (Murray Wisell/Edward Lisbona)
In Your Arms (Aaron Schroeder/Wally Gold)
Give Me The Right (Fred Wise/Norman Blagman)
I Feel So Bad (Chuck Willis)
It's A Sin (Fred Rose/Zeb Turner)
I Want You With Me (Woody Harris)
There's Always Me (Don Robertson)
Starting Today (Don Robertson)
Sentimental Me (Jimmy Cassin/Jim Morehead)
Judy (Teddy Redell)
Put The Blame On Me (Twomey/Wise/Blagman)

March 21–23, 1961: Soundtrack Recordings for Paramount's *Blue Hawaii*, Radio Recorders; Hollywood, California

Hawaiian Sunset (Sid Tepper/Roy C. Bennett)
Aloha Oe (Arranged and Adapted by Elvis Presley)
Ku-U-I-Po (Pretti/Creatore/Weiss)
No More (Don Robertson/Hal Blair)
Slicin' Sand (Sid Tepper/Roy C. Bennett)
Blue Hawaii (Lee Robin/Ralph Rainger)
Ito Eats (Sid Tepper/Roy C. Bennett)
Hawaiian Wedding Song (King/Hoffman/Manning)
Island Of Love (Sid Tepper/Roy C. Bennett)
Steppin' Out Of Line (movie version)
    (Wise/Weisman/Fuller)

174

Steppin/ Out Of Line (Wise/Weisman/Fuller)
Almost Always True (Fred Wise/Ben Weisman)
Moonlight Swim (Sylvia Dee/Ben Weisman)
Can't Help Falling In Love (movie version)
     (Perett/Creatore/Weiss)
Can't Help Falling In Love (Perett/Creatore/Weiss)
Beach Boy Blues (Sid Tepper/Roy C. Bennett)
Beach Boy Blues (movie version) (Sid Tepper/
     Roy C. Bennett)
Rock-A-Hula Baby (Wise/Weisman/Fuller)

In three days, Elvis recorded 15 songs for the film *Blue Hawaii*. Two days later, he was in Hawaii for a press conference and benefit concert on March 25. Over $62,000 was raised for building a memorial to the entombed sailors of the USS Arizona in Pearl Harbor. Principle photography for *Blue Hawaii* began on March 27th.

March 25, 1961: Live Recordings, Bloch Arena; Pearl Harbor, Hawaii

Heartbreak Hotel (Axton/Durden/Presley)
All Shook Up (Blackwell/Presley)
(Now And Then There's) A Fool Such As I
     (Bill Trader/Bob Miller)
I Got A Woman (Ray Charles)
Love Me (Jerry Leiber/Mike Stoller)
Such A Night (Lincoln Chase)
Reconsider Baby (Lowell Fulsom)
I Need Your Love Tonight (Sid Wayne/Bix Reichner)
That's All Right (Arthur Crudup)
Don't Be Cruel (Blackwell/Presley)
One Night (Barholomew/King)
Are You Lonesome Tonight? (Roy Turk/Lou Handman)
It's Now Or Never (Aaron Schroeder/Wally Gold)

Swing Down Sweet Chariot (Traditional/arranged by
 Elvis Presley)
Hound Dog (Jerry Leiber/Mike Stoller)

June 25, 1961: Studio Sessions for RCA, RCA's Studio B; Nashville, Tennessee

Kiss Me Quick (Doc Pomus/Mort Shuman)
That's Someone You Never Forget (Red West/
 Elvis Presley)
I'm Yours (Don Robertson)
(Marie's The Name Of) His Latest Flame (Doc Pomus/
 Mort Shuman)
Little Sister (Doc Pomus/Mort Shuman)

July 2, 1961: Soundtrack Recordings for Mirisch Company's *Follow That Dream*, RCA's Studio B; Nashville, Tennessee

Angel (Sid Tepper/Roy C. Bennett)
Follow That Dream (Fred Wise/Ben Weisman)
What A Wonderful Life (Sid Wayne/Jerry Livingston)
I'm Not The Marrying Kind (Mack David/Sherman
 Edwards)
Sound Advice (Giant/Baum/Kaye)

October 15, 1961: Studio Sessions for RCA, RCA's Studio B; Nashville, Tennessee

For The Millionth And The Last Time (Roy C.
 Bennett/Sid Tepper)
Good Luck Charm (Aaron Schroeder/Wally Gold)
Anything That's Part Of You (Don Robertson)
I Met Her Today (Don Robertson/Hal Blair)
Night Rider (Doc Pomus/Mort Shuman)

October 26–27, 1961: Soundtrack Recordings for Mirisch Company's *Kid Galahad*, Radio Recorders; Hollywood, California

King Of The Whole Wide World (Ruth
    Batchelor/Bob Roberts)
A Whistling Tune (Sherman Edwards/Hal David)
Home Is Where The Heart Is (Sherman Edwards/
    Hal David)
Riding The Rainbow (Ben Weisman/Fred Wise)
Riding The Rainbow (Ben Weisman/Fred Wise)
I Got Lucky (Fuller/Weisman/Wise)
I Got Lucky (Fuller/Weisman/Wise)
This Is Living (Ben Weisman/Fred Wise)
King Of The Whole Wide World (Ruth Batchelor/
    Bob Roberts)

Recorded in March, the soundtrack for *Blue Hawaii* was released in October. The LP went to number one, sold over two million copies in the first year, and became the biggest selling album of Elvis' lifetime.

For the first time in a year, Elvis was back at number one on the charts with the appropriately titled 'Good Luck Charm' and its flip side 'Anything That's Part of You', released in February 1962. The single sold less than a million copies.

March 18–19, 1962: Studio Sessions for RCA, RCA's Studio B; Nashville, Tennessee

Something Blue (Paul Evans/Al Byron)
Gonna Get Back Home Somehow (Doc Pomus/
    Mort Shuman)
(Such An) Easy Question (Otis Blackwell/
    Winfield Scott)
Fountain Of Love (Bill Giant/Jeff Lewis)

Just For Old Time Sake (Sid Tepper/Roy C. Bennett)
Night Rider (Doc Pomus/Mort Shuman)
You'll Be Gone (Red West/E. Presley/Charlie Hodge)
I Feel That I've Known You Forever (Doc Pomus/
    Alan Jeffreys)
Just Tell Her Jim Said Hello (Mike Stoller/Jerry Leiber)
Suspicion (Doc Pomus/Mort Shuman)
She's Not You (Doc Pomus/Mike Stoller/Jerry Leiber)

March 26–28, 1962: Soundtrack Recordings for Paramount's *Girls! Girls! Girls!*, Radio Recorders; Hollywood, California

March 26

I Don't Want To (Janice Tarre/Fred Spielman)
We're Comin' In Loaded (Otis Blackwell/
    Winfield Scott)
Thanks To The Rolling Sea (Ruth Batchelor/
    Bob Roberts)
Where Do You Come From (Ruth Batchelor/
    Bob Roberts)
Girls! Girls! Girls! (J. Leiber/M. Stoller)
Return to Sender (Otis Blackwell/Winfield Scott)
Because Of Love (Ruth Batchelor/Bob Roberts)

March 27

The Walls Have Ears (Roy C. Bennett/Sid Tepper)
A Boy Like Me, A Girl Like You (Sid Tepper/
    Roy C. Bennett)

March 28

Mama (Charles O'Curran/Dudley Brooks)
Earth Boy (Sid Tepper/Roy C. Bennett)
Earth Boy (movie version) (Sid Tepper/Roy C. Bennett)

Dainty Little Moonbeams (Unknown)
I Don't Wanna Be Tied (Giant/Baum/Kaye)
Plantation Rock (Giant/Baum/Kaye)

Day Unknown

We'll Be Together (Charles O'Curran/Dudley Brooks)

The five songs recorded for the film *Follow That Dream* were combined with an unreleased track from *Blue Hawaii* and four cuts from the March 1962 sessions to make the aptly titled *Pot Luck*. Shipped in June, the album rose to number four on the charts and sold around 300,000 copies.

August 30, 1962: Soundtrack Recordings for MGM's *It Happened At The World's Fair*, Radio Recorders; Hollywood, California

Take Me To The Fair (Sid Tepper/Roy C. Bennett)
Happy Ending (Ben Weisman/Sid Wayne)
Happy Ending (movie version) (Ben Weisman/
    Sid Wayne)
Relax (Sid Tepper/Roy C. Bennett)

September 22, 1962: Soundtrack Recordings for MGM's *It Happened At The World's Fair*, Radio Recorders; Hollywood, California

I'm Falling In Love Tonight (Don Robertson)
They Remind Me Too Much Of You (Don
    Robertson)
Cotton Candy Land (Ruth Batchelor/Bob Roberts)
A World Of Our Own (Giant/Baum/Kaye)
How Would You Like To Be (Ben Raleigh/
    Mark Barkan)
One Broken Heart For Sale (movie version)
    (Otis Blackwell/ Winfield Scott)

One Broken Heart For Sale (Otis Blackwell/
    Winfield Scott)
Beyond The Bend (Ben Weisman/Fred Wise/
    Dee Fuller)
Take Me To The Fair (Sid Tepper/Roy C. Bennett)

Released in October, 'Return to Sender'/'Where Do You Come From?' reached number two on *Billboard*'s Top 100 chart, and in the UK hit number one, where it remained for three weeks. The soundtrack for *Girls! Girls! Girls!* was shipped in November. Although it reached number three on the charts, the album had far fewer sales than the successful *Blue Hawaii* soundtrack, moving less than 600,000 copies.

January 22–23, 1963: Soundtrack Sessions for Paramount's *Fun In Acapulco*, Radio Recorders; Hollywood, California

January 22

Bossa Nova Baby (Jerry Leiber/Mike Stoller)
I Think I'm Gonna Like It Here (Don Robertson/
    Hal Blair)
Mexico (Sid Tepper/Roy C. Bennett)
Marguerita (Don Robertson)
Vino, Dinero Y Amor (Sid Tepper/Roy C. Bennett)

January 23

(There's) No Room To Rhumba In A Sports Car
    (Fred Wise/Dick Manning)
Fun In Acapulco (Ben Weisman/Sid Wayne)
El Toro (Giant/Baum/Kaye)
I Think I'm Gonna Like It Here (remake) (Don
    Robertson/Hal Blair)
The Bullfighter Was A Lady (remake) (Sid Tepper/
    Roy C. Bennett)

You Can't Say No In Acapulco (S. Feller/D. Fuller/
  L. Morris)
Guadalajara (Pepe Guisar)

May 26–27, 1963: Studio Sessions for RCA, RCA's Studio B; Nashville, Tennessee

May 26

Echoes Of Love (Bob Roberts/Paddy McMains)
Please Don't Drag That String Around (Otis
  Blackwell/Winfield Scott)
(You're The) Devil In Disguise (Giant/Baum/Kaye)
Never Ending (Buddy Kaye/Phil Springer)
What Now, What Next, Where To (Don
  Robertson/Hal Blair)
Witchcraft (Dave Bartholomew/P. King)
Finders Keepers, Losers Weepers (Dory Jones/
  Ollie Jones)
Love Me Tonight (Don Robertson)

May 27

Memphis Tennessee (Chuck Berry)
(It's A) Long Lonely Highway (Doc Pomus/
  Mort Shuman)
Ask Me (Modugno/Giant/Baum/Kaye)
Western Union (Sid Tepper/Roy C. Bennett)
Slowly But Surely (Sid Wayne/Ben Weisman)
Blue River (Paul Evans/Fred Tobias)

Recorded in May, '(You're The) Devil In Disguise' with B-side
'Please Don't Drag That String Around' was the first single to
be released in quite some time that had not come from a movie.
Shipped in June, it reached number three on the charts and sold
around 700,000 units. With sales of non-soundtrack albums in
decline, the album that was to be made up of other songs from

the May sessions was scrapped. Two of the songs were later used as bonus tracks on the *Fun In Acapulco* soundtrack album released in November.

July 9–11 and August 30, 1963: Soundtrack Recordings for MGM's *Viva Las Vegas*, Radio Recorders; Hollywood, California

July 9

Night Life (Giant/Baum/Kaye)
C'mon Everybody (Joy Byers)
If You Think I Don't Need You (Red West/
    Joe Cooper)

July 10

Viva Las Vegas (Doc Pomus/Mort Shuman)
I Need Somebody To Lean On (Doc Pomus/
    Mort Shuman)
Do The Vega (Giant/Baum/Kaye)
Santa Lucia (arranged by Elvis Presley)
Yellow Rose Of Texas/The Eyes Of Texas
    (Wise/Starr)
C'mon Everybody (movie version) (Joy Byers)

July 11

The Lady Loves Me (Sid Tepper/Roy C. Bennett)
You're The Boss (Jerry Leiber/Mike Stoller)
Today, Tomorrow And Forever (duet)
    (Giant/Baum/Kaye)
Today, Tomorrow And Forever (Giant/Baum/Kaye)

August 30

What'd I Say (Ray Charles)

September 29–30, 1963: Soundtrack Recordings for MGM's *Kissin' Cousins*, RCA's Studio B; Nashville, Tennessee

September 29

There's Gold In The Mountains (Giant/Baum/Kaye)
One Boy, Two Little Girls (Giant/Baum/Kaye)
Once Is Enough (Sid Tepper/Roy C. Bennett)
Tender Feeling (Giant/Baum/Kaye)
Kissin' Cousins No. 2 (Giant/Baum/Kaye)

September 30

Smokey Mountain Boy (Rosenblatt/Millrose)
Catchin' On Fast (Giant/Baum/Kaye)
Barefoot Ballad (Dolores Fuller/Lee Morris)
Anyone (Could Fall In Love With You)
     (Benjamin/Marcus/DeJesus)
Kissin' Cousins (Fred Wise/Randy Starr)

October 10, 1963: Soundtrack Recordings for MGM's *Kissin' Cousins*, MGM Studios; Culver City, California

Elvis overdubbed vocals for the September 29–30, 1963
     recordings

January 12, 1964: Studio Sessions for RCA, RCA's Studio B; Nashville, Tennessee

Memphis Tennessee (Chuck Berry)
Ask Me (Modugno/Giant/Baum/Kaye)
It Hurts Me (Joy Byers/Charles E. Daniels)

To promote the March premiere of *Kissin' Cousins*, the single 'Kissin' Cousins'/'It Hurts Me' was released in February 1964. The single rose to number 12 and sold 700,000 copies. The soundtrack album was released in March, with two bonus tracks from the May 1963 sessions. The LP went to number six on the charts and sold 300,000 units. In April, two more singles were released. 'Kiss Me Quick' with 'Suspicion' from the 1963 *Pot Luck* album, stalled at number 34 and sold just over 200,000 copies, making it Elvis' worst selling single to date. The other release, 'What'd I Say'/'Viva Las Vegas' did better, reaching number 21 and selling half a million copies, but it was the poorest showing to date for previously unreleased material. The *Viva Las Vegas* soundtrack, released in May, was also met with declining enthusiasm, selling only 150,000 copies, and was shot down at number 92.

March 2–3, April 29, and May 14, 1964: Soundtrack Sessions for Paramount's *Roustabout*, Radio Recorders; Hollywood, California

March 2

Little Egypt (Leiber/Stoller)
Poison Ivy League (Giant/Baum/Kaye)
Hard Knocks (Joy Byers)
It's A Wonderful World (Sid Tepper/Roy C. Bennett)

March 3

Big Love Big Heartache (Dee Fuller/Les Morris/
   Sonny Hendix)
One Track Heart (Giant/Baum/Kaye)
Roustabout (Otis Blackwell/Winfield Scott)
It's Carnival Time (Ben Weisman/Sid Wayne)
Carny Town (Fred Wise/Randy Starr)
There's A Brand New Day On The Horizon (Joy Byers)
Wheels On My Heels (Sid Tepper/Roy C. Bennett)

April 29

Roustabout (Giant/Baum/Kaye)

May 14

Roustabout (overdubbed vocals) (Giant/Baum/Kaye)

June 10–12 and 15, 1964: Soundtrack Sessions for MGM's *Girl Happy*, Radio Recorders; Hollywood, California

June 10

Puppet On A String (Sid Tepper/Roy C. Bennett)
The Meanest Girl In Town (Joy Byers)
Girl Happy (Doc Pomus/Norman Meadse)

June 11

Cross My Heart And Hope To Die (Sid Wayne/
    Ben Weisman)
Spring Fever (Giant/Baum/Kaye)
Do Not Disturb (Giant/Baum/Kaye)
I've Got To Find My Baby (Joy Byers)
Fort Lauderdale Chamber Of Commerce (Sid Tepper/
    Roy C. Bennett)

June 12

Startin' Tonight (L. Rosenblatt/V. Williams)
Do The Clam (S. Wayne/B. Weisman/S. Fuller)
Wolf Call (Giant/Baum/Kaye)

June 15 – Elvis overdubbed vocals for:

Cross My Heart And Hope To Die (Sid Wayne/
    Ben Weisman)
Fort Lauderdale Chamber Of Commerce (Sid Tepper/
    Roy C. Bennett)
Startin' Tonight (L. Rosenblatt/V. Williams)
Do The Clam (S. Wayne/B. Weisman/S. Fuller)
Wolf Call (Giant/Baum/Kaye)

Over the past two years, Elvis had rarely set foot in a studio to record anything but soundtrack albums. The July 1964 single release 'Such A Night' was pulled from the 1960's album *Elvis Is Back,* and coupled with 'Never Ending' from his May 1963 recording sessions. The single did well, however, climbing to number 16 and selling more than 300,000 copies.

February 24–26, 1965: Soundtrack Sessions for MGM's *Harum Scarum*, RCA's Studio B; Nashville, Tennessee

February 24

Shake That Tambourine (Giant/Baum/Kaye)

February 25

So Close, Yet So Far (From Paradise) (Joy Byers)
My Desert Serenade (Stanley Gelber)
Wisdom Of The Ages (Giant/Baum/Kaye)
Kismet (Sid Tepper/Roy C. Bennett)
Hey Little Girl (Joy Byers)

February 26

Golden Coins (Giant/Baum/Kaye)
Animal Instinct (Giant/Baum/Kaye)
Harem Holiday (P. Andreoli/V. Poncia, Jr/J. Crane)
Go East, Young Man (Giant/Baum/Kaye)
Mirage (Giant/Baum/Kaye)

May 12–14, 1965: Soundtrack Sessions for United Artists' *Frankie and Johnny*, Radio Recorders; Hollywood, California

May 12

Come Along (David Hess)
Beginner's Luck (Sid Tepper/Roy C. Bennett)

Down By The Riverside/When The Saints Go
Marching In (Giant/Baum/Kaye)

May 13

Please Don't Stop Loving Me (Joy Byers)
Shout It Out (Giant/Baum/Kaye)
Frankie And Johnny (movie version) (A/ Gottlieb/
F. Karger/B. Weisman)
What Every Woman Lives For (Doc Pomus/
Mort Shuman)
Hard Luck (Ben Weisman/Sid Wayne)

May 14

Petunia, The Gardener's Daughter (Sid Tepper/
Roy C. Bennett)
Look Out, Broadway (Fred Wise/Randy Starr)
Everybody Come Aboard (Giant/Baum/Kaye)
Chesay (Fred Karger/Ben Weisman/Sid Wayne)
Frankie And Johnny (A. Gottlieb/F. Karger/
B. Weisman)

July 26–27 and August 2–4, 1965: Soundtrack Sessions for Paramount's *Paradise, Hawaiian Style*, Radio Recorders; Hollywood, California

July 26

Drums Of The Island (Polynesian Culture/Tepper/
Bennett)
Datin' (Fred Wise/Randy Starr)
Scratch My Back (Giant/Baum/Kaye)

July 27

Stop Where You Are (Giant/Baum/Kaye)
A Dog's Life (Sid Wayne/Ben Weisman)
This Is My Heaven (Giant/Baum/Kaye)

Paradise, Hawaiian Style (Giant/Baum/Kaye)
House Of Sand (Giant/Baum/Kaye)
Queenie Wahine's Papaya (Giant/Baum/Kaye)

August 2

Sand Castles (Herb Goldberg/David Hess)

Even though sales on Elvis' records had dropped 40 per cent over the past five years, Colonel Parker negotiated a deal with RCA in October 1965 for better royalty rates and advances, extending the contract to 1972, with a two-year option. That same month, 'Puppet On A String' was released with B-side 'Wooden Heart', which was pulled from the *G.I. Blues* soundtrack that had been released five years earlier. It was the second time in a year that this song had been used as a B-side, the result of RCA's efforts to recoup some of the money spent to secure the right to release it internationally. The single made it to number 14 on the charts. A holiday single was also released in October, 'Santa Claus Is Back In Town' with flip side 'Blue Christmas' from *Elvis' Christmas Album*. Although the record did not chart, it sold almost a million copies.

February 16–17, 1966: Soundtrack Recordings for MGM's *Spinout*, Radio Recorders; Hollywood, California

February 16

Smorgasbord (Sid Tepper/Roy C. Bennett)
Stop, Look And Listen (Joy Byers)
Am I Ready (Sid Tepper/Roy C. Bennett)
Beach Shack (Giant/Baum/Kaye)

February 17

Never Say Yes (Doc Pomus/Mort Shuman)
Spinout (Sid Wayne/Ben Weisman/Dee Fuller)

All That I Am (Sid Tepper/Roy C. Bennett)
Adam And Evil (Fred Wise/Randy Starr)
I'll Be Back (Sid Wayne/Ben Weisman)

February 1966 – early 1967: Home Recordings, Rocca Place; Hollywood, California

After Loving You (E. Miller/J. Lantz)
If I Love You (Oscar Hammerstein/Richard Rodgers)
Beyond The Reef (J. Pitman)
Show Me Thy Ways, O Lord (Hazel Shade)
Tumblin' Tumbleweeds (Bob Nolan)
Hide Thou Me (Lowry/Crosby)
It's No Fun Being Lonely (Red West)
San Antonio Rose (Bob Wills)
Tennessee Waltz (Redd Stewart/Pee Wee King)
Mary Lou Brown (Red West)
Moonlight Sonata (Beethoven)
Oh How I Love Jesus (Traditional)
I, John (incomplete) (William Gaither)
Suppose (S. Dee/G. Goehring)
Fools Rush In (R. Bloom/J. Mercer)
It's A Sin To Tell A Lie (Billy Mayhew)
What Now My Love (Sigman/Becaud)
500 Miles (West)
Blowin' In The Wind (Dylan)
Be My Love (Sammy Cahn/Nicholas Brodszky)
Baby What You Want Me To Do (Jimmy Reed)
Write To Me From Naples (A/ Alstone/J. Kennedy)
My Heart Cries For You (P. Faith/C. Sigman)
Dark Moon (N. Miller)

Principle photography for *Spinout* began on February 21, 1966. Elvis had been trying out different musical styles and had become particularly intrigued by folk music, listening to songs by Peter, Paul and Mary, Ian and Sylvia, and Bob Dylan. This was reflected in his choice of songs to record, including the Dylan-penned 'Blowin' In The Wind' and 'Tomorrow Is A Long Time'.

May 25–28, 1966: Studio Sessions for RCA, RCA's Studio B; Nashville, Tennessee

May 25

Run On (arranged by Elvis Presley)
How Great Thou Art (Stuart K. Hine)
Stand By Me (arranged by Elvis Presley)
Where No One Stands Alone (Mosie Lister)
Down In The Alley (Jesse Stone and the Clovers)
Tomorrow Is A Long Time (Bob Dylan)

May 26

Love Letters (E. Heyman/V. Young)
So High (Arranged by Elvis Presley)
Farther Along (arranged by Elvis Presley)
By And By (arranged by Elvis Presley)
In The Garden (C. A. Miles)
Beyond The Reef (J. Pitman)

May 27

Somebody Bigger Than You And I (J. Lange/
     H. Heath/S. Burke)
Without Him (Mylon LeFevre)
If The Lord Wasn't Walking By My Side
     (Henry Slaughter)
Where Could I Go But To The Lord (J. B. Coats)
Come What May (Tableporter)
Fools Fall In Love (J. Leiber/M. Stoller)

June 10–12, 1966: Studio Sessions for RCA, RCA's Studio B; Nashville, Tennessee

Indescribably Blue (Darrell Glenn)
I'll Remember You (Kuiokalani Lee)
If Every Day Was Like Christmas (Red West)

June 28, 1966: Soundtrack Sessions for MGM's *Double Trouble*, Radio Recorders; Hollywood, California

City By Night (Giant/Baum/Kaye)
Could I Fall In Love (Randy Starr)
There's So Much World To See (Sid Tepper/
    Ben Weisman)
There's So Much World To See (Sid Tepper/
    Ben Weisman)
Long Legged Girl (With The Short Dress On)

June 29–30, 1966: Soundtrack Sessions for MGM's *Double Trouble*, MGM Studios Recording Stage; Hollywood, California

Double Trouble (Doc Pomus/Mort Shuman)
Baby, If You'll Give Me All Of Your Love (Joy Byers)
I Love Only One Girl (Sid Tepper/Roy C. Bennett)
It Won't Be Long (Sid Wayne/Ben Weisman)
Old McDonald (Randy Starr)
Long Legged Girl (With The Short Dress On)
    (J. L. MacFarland/W. Scott)

September 28–29, 1966: Soundtrack Sessions for Paramount's *Easy Game, Easy Go*, Paramount Studio Recording Stage; Hollywood, California

September 28

Easy Come, Easy Go (Ben Weisman/Sid Wayne)

I'll Take Love (Dolores Fuller/Mark Barkan)
Sing You Children (Gerald Nelson/Fred Burch)

September 29

She's A Machine (movie version) (Joy Byers)
She's A Machine (Joy Byers)
The Love Machine (G. Nelson/F. Burch/C. Taylor)
Yoga Is As Yoga Does (Gerald Nelson/Fred Burch)
You Gotta Stop (Giant/Baum/Kaye)

With the inclusion of three bonus tracks not from the film, the soundtrack album for *Spinout* was more up-tempo than Elvis' recent releases. The October 1966 released LP climbed to number 18 on the charts and sold marginally better than Elvis' two previous soundtrack albums, topping out around 300,000 units sold. The single 'Spinout'/'All That I Am' failed to help drive sales as well, scoring an all-time low for a non–seasonal release at number 40.

In November, RIAA certifies the LP *Elvis Presley* Platinum for a million copies sold.

February 21–23, 1967: Soundtrack Recordings for United Artists' *Clambake*, RCA's Studio B; Nashville, Tennessee

February 21

The Girl I Never Loved (Randy Starr)
How Can You Lose What You Never Had
(Ben Weisman/ Sid Wayne)
You Don't Know Me (Walker/Arnold)
A House That Has Everything (Sid Tepper/
Roy C. Bennett)

February 22

Who Needs Money (Randy Starr)

Confidence (Sid Tepper/Roy C. Bennett)
Hey, Hey, Hey (Joy Byers)
Clambake (Ben Weisman/Sid Wayne)

February 23

Clambake (reprise) (Ben Weisman/Sid Wayne)

Elvis' love of gospel music was ignited in his early years. The February 1967 release of his gospel album *How Great Thou Art* showcased that passion. The LP sold just 200,000 copies, but was critically acclaimed and earned Elvis his first Grammy Award from the National Academy of Recording Arts and Sciences (NARAS) for Best Sacred Performance for 'How Great Thou Art'.

March 26, 1967: Studio Session for RCA, RCA's Studio B; Nashville, Tennessee

Suppose (Sylvia Dee/George Goehring)

June 20–21, 1967: Soundtrack Recordings for MGM's *Speedway*, MGM Studios; Hollywood, California

June 20

There Ain't Nothing Like A Song (Joy Byers/
    Bob Johnston)
Your Time Hasn't Come Yet Baby (movie version)
    (Hirschhorn/Kasha)
Five Sleepy Heads (Sid Tepper/Roy C. Bennett)
Who Are You? (Sid Wayne/Ben Weisman)
Speedway (Glazer/Schlaks)
Suppose (long version) (Slyvia Dee/George Goehring)
Suppose (short version) (Slyvia Dee/George Goehring)

June 21

Let Yourself Go (Joy Byers)

He's Your Uncle Not Your Dad (Sid Wayne/
   Ben Weisman)

September 10–11, 1967: Studio Sessions for RCA, RCA's Studio B; Nashville, Tennessee

September 10

Guitar Man (Jerry Reed)
Big Boss Man (Smith/Dixon)
Mine (Sid Tepper/Roy C. Bennett)
Singing Tree (A. L. Owens/Solberg)
Just Call Me Lonesome (Griffin)

June 11

Hi-Heel Sneakers (Higginbotham)
You Don't Know Me (Walker/Arnold)
We Call On Him (Fred Karger/Ben Weisman/
   Sid Wayne)
You'll Never Walk Alone (Rodgers/Hammerstein)
Singing Tree (A. L. Owens/Solberg)

October 1, 1967: Soundtrack Recordings for MGM's *Stay Away, Joe*, RCA's Studio B; Nashville, Tennessee

Stay Away, Joe (Ben Weisman/Sid Wayne)
All I Needed Was The Rain (Sid Wayne/Ben Weisman)
Dominick (Sid Wayne/Ben Weisman)

January 15–16, 1968: Soundtrack Recordings for MGM's *Stay Away, Joe*, RCA's Studio B; Nashville, Tennessee

January 15

Too Much Monkey Business (Chuck Berry)
Goin' Home (Joy Byers)

January 16

Stay Away (Sid Tepper/Roy C. Bennett)
U.S. Male (Jerry Reed)

RCA released *Elvis* a collection of recordings that had earned Gold status, volume 4, in February 1968.

March 7, 1968: Soundtrack Sessions for MGM's *Live A Little, Love A Little*, Western Recorders; Hollywood, California

Wonderful World (Fletcher/Flett)
Edge Of Reality (Giant/Baum/Kaye)
A Little Less Conversation (Billy Strange/Mac Davis)
Almost In Love (Bonfa/Starr)

June 20–23, 1968: Studio Recordings for NBC's *Elvis*, Western Recorders; Burbank, California

June 20

Nothingville (Strange/Davis)
Let Youself Go (Joy Byers)
Big Boss Man (Smith/Dixon)
It Hurts Me (Joy Byers/Charlie E. Daniels)

June 21

Guitar Man (evil/live) (Jerry Hubbard)
Little Egypt (Jerry Leiber/Mike Stoller)
Trouble (after Karate/live) (Jerry Leiber/Mike Stoller)
Where Could I Got But To The Lord (J. B. Coats)

June 22

Up Above My Head (W/ Earl Brown)
Saved (Jerry Leiber/Mike Stoller)
Trouble (opening) (Jerry Leiber/Mike Stoller)
Guitar Man (opening) (Jerry Hubbard)

June 23

If I Can Dream (W. Earl Brown)
Memories (Strange/Davis)
A Little Less Conversation (Billy Strange/Mac Davis)

June 24–25, 1968: Rehearsals, Dressing Room at NBC, Burbank, California

June 24

I Got A Woman (Ray Charles)
Blue Moon/Young Love/Happy Day (Rodgers/Hart –
      Carol Joyner/Ric Cartley – unknown)
When It Rains It Really Pours (B. Emerson)
Blue Christmas (Hayes/Johnson)
Are You Lonesome Tonight?/That's My Desire
      (Roy Turk/ Lou Handman – Carroll Loveday/
      Helmy Kresa)
That's When Your Heartaches Begin
      (Raskin/Brown/Fisher)
Love Me (Jerry Leiber/Mike Stoller)
When My Blue Moon Turns To Gold Again
      (Walker/Sullivan)
Blue Christmas/Santa Claus Is Back In Town
      (Hayes/Johnson – Jerry Leiber/Mike Stoller)

June 25

Danny Boy (Weatherly)
Baby What You Want Me To Do (J. Reed)
Love Me (Jerry Leiber/Mike Stoller)
Tiger Man (S. Burns/J. H. Louis)
Santa Claus Is Back In Town (Jerry Leiber/
      Mike Stoller)
Lawdy, Miss Clawdy (Lloyd Price)
One Night (Bartholomew/King)

Blue Christmas (Hayes/Johnson)
Baby What You Want Me To Do (J. Reed)
When My Blue Moon Turns To Gold Again
    (Walker/Sullivan)
Blue Moon Of Kentucky (Bill Monroe)

June 27, 1968: Live Recordings for NBC, NBC Studios; Burbank, California

That's All Right (Crudup)
Heartbreak Hotel (Axton/Durden/Presley)
Love Me (Leiber/Stoller)
Baby What You Want Me To Do (J. Reed)
Blue Suede Shoes (Carl Perkins)
Baby What You Want Me To Do (J. Reed)
Lawdy, Miss Clawdy (Lloyd Price)
Are You Lonesome Tonight? (Roy Turk/
    Lou Handman)
When My Blue Moon Turns To Gold Again
    (Walker/Sullivan)
Blue Christmas (Johnson/Hayes)
Trying To Get To You (McCoy/Singleton)
One Night (Bartholomew/King)
Baby What You Want Me To Do (J. Reed)
One Night (Bartholomew/King)
Memories (Strange/Davis)
Heartbreak Hotel (Axton/Durden/Presley)
Baby What You Want Me To Do (J. Reed)
That's All Right (Crudup)
Are You Lonesome Tonight? (Roy Turk/
    Lou Handman)
Baby What You Want Me To Do (J. Reed)
Blue Suede Shoes (Carl Perkins)
One Night (Bartholomew/King)

Love Me (Jerry Leiber/Mike Stoller)
Trying To Get To You (McCoy/Singleton)
Lawdy, Miss Clawdy (Lloyd Price)
Santa Claus Is Back In Town (Jerry Leiber/Mike Stoller)
Blue Christmas (Johnson/Hayes)
Tiger Man (Burns/Louis)
When My Blue Moon Turns To Gold Again
    (Walker/Sullivan)
Memories (Strange/Davis)

June 29, 1968: Live Recordings for NBC (Arena Segment), NBC Studios; Burbank, California

Heartbreak Hotel (Axton/Durden/Presley)
One Night (Bartholomew/King)
Heartbreak Hotel (Axton/Durden/Presley)
Hound Dog (Jerry Leiber/Mike Stoller)
All Shook Up (Blackwell/Presley)
Can't Help Falling In Love (Peretti/Creatore/Weiss)
Jailhouse Rock (Jerry Leiber/Mike Stoller)
Don't Be Cruel (Blackwell/Presley)
Blue Suede Shoes (Carl Perkins)
Love Me Tender (Presley/Matson)
Trouble/Guitar Man (Jerry Leiber/Mike Stoller –
    Jerry Hubbard)
Baby What You Want Me To Do (J. Reed)
Heartbreak Hotel (Axton/Durden/Presley)
Hound Dog (Leiber/Stoller)
All Shook Up (Blackwell/Presley)
Can't Help Falling In Love (Peretti/Creatore/Weiss)
Jailhouse Rock (Jerry Leiber/Mike Stoller)
Don't Be Cruel (Blackwell/Presley)
Blue Suede Shoes (Carl Perkins)
Love Me Tender (Presley/Matson)

198

Trouble (Jerry Leiber/Mike Stoller)
Trouble/Guitar Man (Jerry Leiber/Mike Stoller –
Jerry Hubbard)

October 15, 1968: Soundtrack Recordings for National Generals' *Charro!*, Samuel Goldwyn Studio; Hollywood, California

Let's Forget About The Stars (A. L. Owens)
Charro! (Mac Davis/Billy Strange)

October 23, 1968: Soundtrack Recordings for MGM's (Jerry Leiber/Mike Stoller) *The Trouble With Girls*, United Artist Recorders; Hollywood, California

Clean Up Your Own Back Yard (Mac Davis/
Billy Strange)
Swing Down Sweet Chariot (Arranged by Elvis Presley)
Signs Of The Zodiac (B. Kaye/B. Weisman)
Almost (B. Kaye/B. Weisman)
The Whiffenpoof Song (Galloway/Minnigerode/
Pomeroy)
Violet (Dueker/P. Lohstroh)

Sales of Elvis' records had dropped appreciably, but the 1968 NBC special *Elvis,* dubbed the 'Comeback Special', soon turned that around. RCA rushed *Elvis,* the album from the special, and the single 'If I Can Dream'/'Edge Of Reality' into stores just prior to the December 3, 1968 airing. 'If I Can Dream' was written specifically to be the show's closing number and proved to be a dramatic climax. Dressed in a white suit, standing before giant red-lighted letters spelling out his name, Elvis belted out the number as only he could, leaving no doubt that he was back. The success of the special drove the single to number 12 with sales of around 800,000, and the LP to number eight with sales over 500,000. The special proved to be a pivotal point in Elvis' career, putting him back on top as a recording artist and performer.

January 13–16 and 20–23, 1969: Studio Sessions for RCA, American Studios; Memphis, Tennessee

January 13

Long Black Limousine (Vern Stovall/Bobby George)
This Is The Story (Arnold/Morrow/Martin)
Wearin' That Loved On Look (Dallas Frazier/
    A. L. Owens)

January 14

You'll Think Of Me (Mort Shuman)
A Little Bit Of Green (Arnold/Morrow/Martin)
I'm Movin' On (Clarence E. Snow)
Gentle On My Mind (John Hartford)

January 15

Don't Cry Daddy (Mac Davis)
Inherit The Wind (Eddie Rabbitt)
Mama Liked The Roses (John Christopher)

January 16

My Little Friend (Shirl Milete)

January 20

In The Ghetto (Mac Davis)
Rubberneckin' (Dory Jones/Bunny Warren)
Gentle On My Mind (vocal overdub) (John Hartford)

January 21

Hey Jude (John Lennon/Paul McCartney)
From A Jack To A King (Ned Miller)

January 22

I'll Hold You In My Heart (Dilback/Horton/Arnold)
Without Love (Danny Small)
I'll Be There (Bobby Darin)
Suspicious Minds (Mark James)

February 17–22, 1969: Studio Sessions for RCA, American Studios; Memphis, Tennessee

February 17

It's My Way/This Time/I Can't Stop Loving You
(Pierce/Walker – Chips Moman/Dob Gibson)
True Love Travels On A Gravel Road (A. L. Owens/
Dallas Frazier)
Stranger In My Own Home Town (Piercy Mayfield)
And The Grass Won't Pay No Mind (Neil Diamond)

February 18

Power Of My Love (Giant/Baum/Kaye)
After Loving You (E. Miller/J. Lantz)
Do You Know Who I Am (Bobby Russell)

February 19

Kentucky Rain (E. Rabbit)
Only The Strong Survive (Gamble/Huff/Butler)

February 20

It Keeps Right On A-Hurtin' (Johnny Tillotson)
Any Day Now (Bob Hilliard/Burt Bacharach)
If I'm A Fool (For Loving You) (Stan Kesler)

February 21

The Fair Is Moving On (Fletcher/Flett)
Who Am I? (Charles Rusty Goodman)

March 5–6, 1969: Soundtrack Recordings for Universal's *Change Of Habit*, Decca Universal Studio; Hollywood, California

> Change Of Habit (Buddy Kaye/Ben Weisman)
> Let's Be Friends (Arnold/Morrow/Martin)
> Let Us Pray (Buddy Kaye/Ben Weisman)
> Have A Happy (Weisman/Fuller/Kaye)

Released in March, in time for Easter, 'His Hand In Mine' was pulled from the 1960 gospel album *His Hand In Mine* and paired with flip side "How Great Thou Art", the title cut from the 1967 gospel LP.

The first release from the American sessions, 'In The Ghetto'/ 'Any Day Now', shipped in April 1969, rose to number three on the charts and sold 1.2 million copies.

August 21–26, 1969: Live Recordings for RCA; The International Hotel, Las Vegas, Nevada

August 21–26, Specifics Unknown

> Memories (Billy Strange/Mac Davis)

August 21 – Midnight Show

> Reconsider Baby (Lowell/Fulson)

August 24 – Dinner Show

> Jailhouse Rock/Don't Be Cruel (Leiber/Stoller)

August 24 – Midnight Show

> I Got A Woman (Ray Charles)
> Johnny B. Goode (Chuck Berry)
> Are You Lonesome Tonight? (Roy Turk/Lou Handman)

August 25 – Dinner Show

> Baby What You Want Me To Do (Jimmy Reed)
> Funny How Time Slips Away (Willie Nelson)

Runaway (Crook/Del Shannon)
Yesterday/Hey Jude (McCartney/Lennon)
In The Ghetto (Scott Davis)

August 25 – Midnight Show

Blue Suede Shoes (Carl Perkins)
All Shook Up (Otis Blackwell/Elvis Presley)
Heartbreak Hotel (Axton/Durden/Presley)
Hound Dog (Jerry Leiber/Mike Stoller)
I Can't Stop Loving You (Don Gibson)
My Babe (W. Dixon)
Mystery Train/Tiger Man (J. H. Louis/S. Burns)
Words (R. B. & M. Gibbs)
What'd I Say (Ray Charles)

August 26 – Dinner Show

Love Me Tender (E. Presley/V. Matson)
Jailhouse Rock/Don't Be Cruel (Jerry Leiber/
    Mike Stoller)
Inherit The Wind (Eddie Rabbitt)
Suspicious Minds (Mark James)
Can't Help Falling In Love (Peretti/Creatore/Weiss)

August 26 – Midnight Show

Are You Lonesome Tonight? (laughing version)
    (Roy Turk/ Lou Handman)
Rubberneckin' (Dory Jones/Bunny Warren)
This Is The Story (Arnold/Morrow/Martin)

'Suspicious Minds'/'You'll Think Of Me' was released in September 1969 and reached number one on *Billboard*'s Top 100 in November. In December, the LP *From Memphis to Vegas/From Vegas to Memphis* was certified Gold by RIAA. The single 'Don't Cry Daddy' peaked at number six, sold a million copies and was certified Gold by RIAA in January 1970.

February 15–19, 1970: Live Recordings for RCA; The International Hotel, Las Vegas, Nevada

February 15–19 – Specifics Unknown

All Shook Up (Otis Blackwell/Elvis Presley)
In The Ghetto (Scott Davis)
Suspicious Minds (Mark James)
I Got A Woman (Ray Charles)
Hound Dog (Jerry Leiber/Mike Stoller)
Long Tall Sally (Richard Penniman/
    Robert Blackwell)
Love Me Tender (E. Presley/V. Matson)
Can't Help Falling In Love (Peretti/Creatore/Weiss)

February 16 – Dinner Show

Proud Mary (John Fogerty)
Sweet Caroline (Neil Diamond)

February 17 – Midnight Show

Don't Cry Daddy (Mac Davis)
Kentucky Rain (E. Rabbitt/D. Heard)
Let It Be Me (Mann Curtis/Pierre Delanoe/
    Gilbert Becaud)

February 18 – Dinner Show

The Wonder Of You (Baker Knight)

February 18 – Midnight Show

Release Me (Miller/Yount/Williams)
See See Rider (Traditional, arranged by Elvis
    Presley)
Polk Salad Annie (Tony Joe White)

February 19 – Midnight Show

Walk A Mile In My Shoes (Joe South)
I Can't Stop Loving You (Don Gibson)

February 18, 1970: Rehearsals for RCA; The International Hotel, Las Vegas, Nevada

The Wonder Of You (Baker Knight)
Release Me (Miller/Young/Williams)
See See Rider (Traditional, arranged by Elvis Presley)

June 4–8, 1970: Studio Sessions for RCA, RCA's Studio B; Nashville, Tennessee

June 4

Twenty Days and Twenty Nights (Weisman/Westlake)
I've Lost You (Howard/Blaikley)
I Was Born About Ten Thousand Years Ago (adapted
    by Elvis Presley)
The Sound Of Your Cry (Giant/Baum/Kaye)
The Fool (Naomi Ford)
A Hundred Years From Now (Lester Flatt/Earl Scruggs)
Little Cabin On The Hill (Bill Monroe/Lester Flatt)
Cindy, Cindy (Kaye/Weisman/Fuller)

June 5

Bridge Over Troubled Water (Paul Simon)
Got My Mojo Working/Keep Your Hands Off Of It
    (Foster – adapted by E. Presley)
How The Web Was Woven (C. Westlake/M. Most)
It's Your Baby, You Rock It (Milete/Fowler)
Stranger In The Crowd (Winfield/Scott)
I'll Never Know (Karger/Wayne/Weisman)
Mary In The Morning (Cymbal/Rashkow)

June 6

I Didn't Make It On Playing Guitar (Elvis Presley)
It Ain't No Big Thing (But It's Growing)
    (Merritt/Joy/Hall)

You Don't Have To Say You Love Me
    (Wickham/Napier)
Just Pretend (D. Flett/G. Fletcher)
This Is Our Dance (Les Reed/Geoff Stephens)
Life (Shirl Milete)
Heart Of Rome (Stephens/Blaikley/Howard)

June 7

When I'm Over You (Shirl Milete)
I Really Don't Want To Know (Barnes/Robertson)
Faded Love (B. Wills/J. Wills)
Tomorrow Never Comes (E. Tubb/Bond)
The Next Step Is Love (Evans/Parnes)
Make The World Go Away (Hank Cochran)
Funny How Time Slips Away (Willie Nelson)
I Washed My Hands In Muddy Water (Joe Babcock)
Love Letters (E. Heymann/V. Young)

June 8

There Goes My Everything (Dallas Frazier)
If I Were You (G. Nelson)
Only Believe (Paul Rader)
Sylvia (Geoff Stephens/Les Reed)
Patch It Up (E. Rabbitt/R. Burke)

July 15, 24, 29, August 4, 7, 1970: Rehearsals for MGM's *That's The Way It Is*, (July 15 and 29) MGM's Soundstage; Hollywood, California; (July 24) RCA's Studios; Hollywood, California; (August 4 and 7): The International Hotel; Las Vegas, Nevada

Stagger Lee (Traditional)
Got My Mojo Working (McKinley/Morganfield/
    Bowman/McShann)
I've Lost You (Howard/Blaikley)

Stranger In The Crowd (Winfield Scott)
The Next Step Is Love (Evans/Parnes)
You Don't Have To Say You Love Me
     (Wickham/Napier)
Sweet Caroline (Neil Diamond)
Yesterday (Lennon/McCartney)
I Can't Stop Loving You (Don Gibson)
Twenty Days And Twenty Nights (Clive Westlake/
     Ben Weisman)
Love Me (Jerry Leiber/Mike Stoller)
Alla En Al Rancho Grande (Silvano Ramos/
     E. D. Urange/J. D. Del Moral)
That's All Right (Arthur Crudup)
Patch It Up (Eddie Rabbitt/Rory Bourke)
Cottonfields (Huddie Ledbetter)
How The Web Was Woven (Clive Westlake/
     Mickey Most)
I Got A Woman (Ray Charles)
The Wonder Of You (Baker Knight)
You've Lost That Lovin' Feelin' (Barry Mann/
     Cynthia Weil)
Something (George Harrison)
Don't Cry Daddy (Mac Davis)
Polk Salad Annie (Tony Joe White)
Bridge Over Troubled Water (Paul Simon)
Just Pretend (G. Fletcher/D. Flatt)
Don't It Make You Wanna Go Home (4 lines only)
     (Joe South)
Love Me Tender (Vera Matson/Elvis Presley)
Words (R. B. & M. Gibb)
Suspicious Minds (Mark James)
I Just Can't Help Believin' (Cynthia Weil/Barry Mann)
Tomorrow Never Comes (Ernest Tubb)
Mary In The Morning (Cymbal/Rashkow)

Heart Of Rome (Stephens/Blaikley/Howard)

Memories (Billy Strange/Mac Davis)

Johnny B. Goode (Chuck Berry)

Make The World Go Away (Hank Cockran)

Stranger In My Own Home Town (Percy Mayfield)

I Washed My Hands In Muddy Water (Joe Babcock)

Little Sister/Get Back (Pomus/Shuman – Lennon/
     McCarthy)

I Was The One (Schroeder/DeMetrius/Blair/Pepper)

Cattle Call (Tex Owens)

Baby Let's Play House (Arthur Gunter)

Don't (Jerry Leiber/Mike Stoller)

Money Honey (Jesse Stone)

(Now And Then There's) A Fool Such As I (Bill Trader)

Froggy Went A-Courtin' (Peretti/Creatore/
     Jimmie Rodgers)

Such A Night (Lincoln Chase)

It's Now Or Never (Schroeder/Gold)

What's I Say (Ray Charles)

The Lord's Prayer (Traditional)

Hava Nagila (Traditional)

My Baby Left Me (Arthur Crudup)

August 10–13, 1970: Live Recordings for RCA and MGM's *That's The Way It Is*; The International Hotel, Las Vegas, Nevada

August 10 – Opening Night Show

The Next Step Is Love (Evans/Parnes)

August 11 – Dinner Show

I've Lost You (Howard/Blaikley)

I Just Can't Help Believin' (Cynthia Weil/Barry Mann)

Bridge Over Troubled Water (Paul Simon)

August 11 – Midnight Show

Something (George Harrison)
Men With Broken Hearts (Hank Williams)
One Night (Bartholomew/King)
Don't Be Cruel (Otis Blackwell/Elvis Presley)
Heartbreak Hotel (Axton/Durden/Presley)

August 12 – Dinner Show

Patch It Up (Eddie Rabbitt/Rory Bourke)
Twenty Days And Twenty Nights (Clive Westlake/
    Ben Weisman)

August 13 – Dinner Show

Don't Cry Daddy (Mac Davis)
In The Ghetto (Mac Davis)
Stranger In The Crowd (Winfield Scott)
Make The World Go Away (Hank Cochran)
Polk Salad Annie (Tony Joe White)
The Wonder Of You (Baker Knight)

August 13 – Midnight Show

You've Lost That Lovin' Feelin' (Cynthia Weil/
    Barry Mann)
Little Sister/Get Back (Pomus/Shuman –
    Lennon/McCartney)
I Was The One (Schroeder/DeMetrius/Blair/Pepper)
Are You Lonesome Tonight? (Roy Turk/Lou
    Handman)

August 10–13 – Specific Show Unknown

That's All Right (Arthur Crudup)
Mystery Train/Tiger Man (Junior Parker/Sam Phillips
    – Joe Hill Louis/Sam Burns)
I Can't Stop Loving You (Don Gibson)
Love Me Tender (Vera Matson/Elvis Presley)

Words (B. M. & R. Gibb)
Sweet Caroline (Neil Diamond)
You Don't Have To Say You Love Me (Wickham
     Napier)
Can't Help Falling In Love (Peretti/Creatore/Weiss)
I Got A Woman (Ray Charles)
Hound Dog (Jerry Leiber/Mike Stoller)
Suspicious Minds (Mark James)
There Goes My Everything (Dallas Frazier)
Just Pretend (Flett/Fletcher)
Walk A Mile In My Shoes (Joe South)
Love Me (Jerry Leiber/Mike Stoller)
Blue Suede Shoes (Carl Perkins)
All Shook Up (Otis Blackwell/Elvis Presley)

September 22, 1970: Studio Sessions for RCA, RCA's Studio B; Nashville, Tennessee

Snowbird (Gene MacLellan)
Where Did They Go, Lord (Dallas Frazier/A. L. Owens)
Whole Lotta Shakin' Goin' On (Dave Williams/
     Sunny David)
Rages To Riches (Richard Adler/Jerry Ross)

'You Don't Have To Say You Love Me', a cover of the Dusty Springfield mega-hit, with B-side 'Patch It Up' was released October 1970 and just missed the Top 10, stalling out at number 11 and selling 800,000 units.

Elvis had a country music following from the beginning of his career when he performed on the Louisiana Hayride. Several of his singles and albums had charted on the country-and-western charts. *Elvis Country*, released in January 1971, honoured those fans. Although the LP was critically accepted, it sold only a half-million copies and peaked at number 12. The single from the album, 'I Really Don't Want To Know'/'There Goes My

Everything' was released at the end of 1970 and did a little better, selling 700,000 copies.

March 15, 1971: Studio Sessions for RCA, RCA's Studio B; Nashville, Tennessee

> The First Time Ever I Saw Your Face (Ewan McColl)
> Amazing Grace (arranged by Elvis Presley)
> Early Morning Rain (Gordon Lightfoot)
> That's What You Get) For Lovin' Me (Gordon Lightfoot)

May 15–21, 1971: Studio Session for RCA, RCA's Studio B; Nashville, Tennessee

May 15

> Miracle Of The Rosary (Lee Denson)
> It Won't Seem Like Christmas (J. A. Balthrop)
> If I Get Home On Christmas Day (Tony McCaulay)
> Padre (LaRue/Hebster/Romans)
> Holly Leaves And Christmas Trees (Red West/
>   Glen Spreen)
> Merry Christmas Baby (L. Baxter/J. Moore)
> Silver Bells (R. Evans/J. Livingston)

May 16

> The Lord's Prayer (arranged by Elvis Presley)
> I'll Be Home On Christmas Day (Michael Jarrett)
> On A Snowy Christmas Night (S. Gelber)
> Winter Wonderland (D. Smith/F. Bernard)
> Don't Think Twice, It's All Right (Bob Dylan)
> O Come, All Ye Faithful (arranged by Elvis Presley)
> The First Noel (arranged by Elvis Presley)
> The Wonderful World Of Christmas (Tobias/Frisch)

May 17

> Help Me Make It Through The Night (Kris Kristofferson)

Until It's Time For You To Go (Buffy Sainte-Marie)
Lady Madonna (John Lennon/Paul McCartney)
Lead Me, Guide Me (D. Akers)

May 18

Fools Rush In (R. Bloom/J. Mercer)
He Touched Me (W. Gaither)
I've Got Confidence (A. Crouch)
An Evening Prayer (Battersby/Gabriel)

May 19

Seeing Is Believing (Red West/Glen Spreen)
A Thing Called Love (Jerry Reed)
It's Still Here (Ivory Joe Hunter)
I'll Take You Home Again Kathleen (arranged by Elvis
    Presley)
I Will Be True (Ivory Joe Hunter)

May 20

I'm Leavin' (Michael Jarrett/Sonny Charles)
We Can Make The Morning (Jay Ramsey)
I Shall Be Released (2 verses only) (Bob Dylan)
It's Only Love (Mark James/Steve Tyrell)

May 21

Love Me, Love The Life I Lead (Tony Macaulay/
    Roger Greenaway)

June 8–10, 1971: Studio Sessions for RCA, RCA's Studio B; Nashville, Tennessee

June 8

Until It's Time For You To Go (remake)
    (Buffy Sainte-Marie)

Put Your Hand In The Hand (Gene Maclellan)
Reach Out To Jesus (Ralph Carmichael)

June 9

He Is My Everything (Dallas Frazier)
There Is No God But God (Bill Kenny)
I, John (Johnson/McFadden/Brooks)
Bosom Of Abraham (Johnson/McFadden/Brooks)

June 10

My Way (Anka/Reveaux/Francois)
I'll Be Home On Christmas Day (remake)
(Michael Jarrett)

February 14–17, 1972: Live Recordings for RCA; The Hilton Hotel, Las Vegas, Nevada

February 14 – Midnight Show

Little Sister/Get Back (Pomus/Shuman)

February 15 – Midnight Show

See See Rider (Traditional; arranged by Elvis Presley)
Proud Mary (J. Fogerty)

February 16 – Midnight Show

Never Been To Spain (Hoyt Axton)
You Gave Me A Mountain (Marty Robbins)
A Big Hunk O' Love (Aaron Schroeder/Sid Wyche)
It's Impossible (Sid Wayne/A. Manzanero)
The Impossible Dream (Mitch Leigh/Joe Darion)
An American Trilogy (Mickey Newbury)

February 17 – Dinner Show

It's Over (Jimmie Rodgers)

Various Shows

Love Me (Jerry Leiber/Mike Stoller)
All Shook Up (Otis Blackwell/Elvis Preseley)
Teddy Bear/Don't Be Cruel (Kal Mann/Bernie Lowe)
Hound Dog (Jerry Leiber/Mike Stoller)
Can't Help Falling In Love (Peretti/Creatore/Weiss)

March 27–29, 1972: Studio Sessions for RCA, RCA's Studio C; Hollywood, California

March 27

Separate Ways (Red West/Richard Mainegra)
For The Good Times (Kris Kristofferson)
Where Do I Go From Here (Paul Williams)

March 28

Burning Love (Dennis Linde)
Fool (Carl Sigman/James Last)

March 29

Always On My Mind (Wayne Carson/Mark James/
	Johnny Christopher)
It's A Matter Of Time (Clive Westlake)

March 30–31 and April 5, 1972: Rehearsals for MGM's *Elvis On Tour*, (March) RCA's Studio C; Hollywood, California, (April) Memorial Auditorium; Buffalo, New York

Burning Love (Dennis Linde)
For The Good Times (Kris Kristofferson)
Johnny B. Goode (Chuck Berry)
A Big Hunk O'Love (Aaron Schroeder/Sid Wyche)

Discography

Always On My Mind (Wayne Carson/Johnny
    Christopher/Mark James)
Separate Ways (Red West/Richard Mainegra)
See See Rider (Traditional/arranged by Elvis Presley)
Never Been To Spain (Hoyt Axton)
Help Me Make It Through The Night
    (Kris Kristofferson)
Proud Mary (John Fogerty)
You Gave Me A Mountain (Marty Robbins)
Until It's Time For You To Go (Buffy Sainte-Marie)
Polk Salad Annie (Tony Joe White)
Love Me (Jerry Leiber/Mike Stoller)
All Shook Up (Otis Blackwell/Elvis Presley)
Heartbreak Hotel (Mae Boren/Tommy Durden/
    Elvis Presley)
(Let Me Be Your) Teddy Bear/Don't Be Cruel
    (Kal Mann/Bernie Lowe – Otis Blackwell/
    Elvis Presley)
The First Time Ever I Saw Your Face (Ewan McColl)
Hound Dog (Jerry Leiber/Mike Stoller)
Release Me (Miller/Stevenson)
Lawdy, Miss Clawdy (Lloyd Price)
Funny How Time Slips Away (Willie Nelson)
I, John (William Gaither)
Bosom Of Abraham (Johnson/McFadden/Brooks)
You Better Run (Traditional/arranged by Elvis Presley)
Lead Me, Guide Me (Doris Akers)
Turn Your Eyes Upon Jesus/Nearer My God To Thee
    (Lemmel/Clarke – Fuller/Adams/Mason)
Bridge Over Troubled Water (Paul Simon)
I'll Remember You (Kuiokalani Lee)
Can't Help Falling In Love (Peretti/Creatore/Weiss)
Young And Beautiful (Silver/Schroeder)

April 9–10, 14, 18, 1972: Live Recordings for RCA and MGM, (April 9) Coliseum; Hampton Roads, Virginia; (April 10) Coliseum; Richmond, Virginia; (April 14) Coliseum; Greensboro, North Carolina; (April 18) Convention Center; San Antonio, Texas

See See Rider (Traditional; arranged by Elvis Presley)

I Got A Woman/Amen (Ray Charles – Traditional; arranged by Elvis Presley)

Proud Mary (John Fogerty)

Never Been To Spain (Hoyt Axton)

You Gave Me A Mountain (Marty Robbins)

Until It's Time For You To Go (Buffy Sainte-Marie)

Polk Salad Annie (Tony Joe White)

Love Me (Jerry Leiber/Mike Stoller)

All Shook Up (Otis Blackwell/Elvis Presley)

Heartbreak Hotel (Mae Boren Axton/Tommy Durden/ Elvis Presley)

(Let Me Be Your) Teddy Bear/Don't Be Cruel (Kal Mann/Bernie Lowe – Otis Blackwell/Elvis Presley)

Are You Lonesome Tonight? (Roy Turk/ Lou Handman)

Hound Dog (Jerry Leiber/Mike Stoller)

Bridge Over Troubled Water (Paul Simon)

It's Over (Jimmie Rodgers)

Love Me Tender (Matson/Presley)

I Can't Stop Loving You (Don Gibson)

Suspicious Minds (Mark James)

For The Good Times (Kris Kristofferson)

An American Trilogy (Mickey Newbury)

How Great Thou Art (Stuart K. Hine)

Burning Love (Dennis Linde)

A Big Hunk O'Love (Aaron Schroeder/Sid Wyche)

Release Me (Miller/Stevenson)

Lawdy, Miss Clawdy (Lloyd Price)
Funny How Time Slips Away (Willie Nelson)
Bridge Over Troubled Water (Paul Simon)
Can't Help Falling In Love (Peretti/Creatore/Weiss)

June 10, 1972: Live Recordings for RCA, Madison Square Garden; New York, New York

Matinee – 2:30 Show

That's All Right (Arthur Crudup)
Proud Mary (John Fogerty)
Never Been To Spain (Hoyt Axton)
You Don't Have To Say You Love Me (Wickham/
     Napier)
Until It's Time For You To Go (Buffy Sainte-Marie)
You've Lost That Lovin' Feelin' (Barry Mann/
     Cynthia Weil)
Polk Salad Annie (Tony Joe White)
Love Me (Jerry Leiber/Mike Stoller)
All Shook Up (Otis Blackwell/Elvis Presley)
Heartbreak Hotel (Mae Boren Axton/Tommy Durden/
     Elvis Presley)
(Let Me Be Your) Teddy Bear/Don't Be Cruel
     (Kal Mann/Bernie Lowe – Otis Blackwell/
     Elvis Presley)
Love Me Tender (Elvis Presley/Vera Matson)
Blue Suede Shoes (Carl Perkins)
Reconsider Baby (Lowell Fulsom)
Hound Dog (Jerry Leiber/Mike Stoller)
I'll Remember You (K. Lee)
Suspicious Minds (Mark James)
For The Good Times (Kris Kristofferson)
An American Trilogy (Mickey Newbury)

Funny How Time Slips Away (Willie Nelson)
I Can't Stop Loving You (Don Gibson)
Can't Help Falling In Love (Peretti/Creatore/Weiss)

Evening – 8.00 p.m. Show

That's All Right (Arthur Crudup)
Proud Mary (John Fogerty)
Never Been To Spain (Hoyt Axton)
You Don't Have To Say You Love Me
    (Wickham/Napier)
You've Lost That Lovin' Feelin' (Barry Mann/
    Cynthia Weil)
Polk Salad Annie (Tony Joe White)
Love Me (Jerry Leiber/Mike Stoller)
All Shook Up (Otis Blackwell/Elvis Presley)
Heartbreak Hotel (Mae Boren Axton/Tommy
    Durden/Elvis Presley)
(Let Me Be Your) Teddy Bear/Don't Be Cruel (Kal
    Mann/Bernie Lowe – Otis Blackwell/Elvis Presley)
Love Me Tender (Elvis Presley/Vera Matson)
The Impossible Dream (The Quest) (Mitch Leigh/
    Joe Darion)
Hound Dog (Jerry Leiber/Mike Stoller)
Suspicious Minds (Mark James)
For The Good Times (Kris Kristofferson)
An American Trilogy (Mickey Newbury)
Funny How Time Slips Away (Willie Nelson)
I Can't Stop Loving You (Don Gibson)
Can't Help Falling In Love (Peretti/Creatore/Weiss)

Just eight days after the successful sold-out concerts at New York's Madison Square Garden, RCA released *Elvis As Recorded At Madison Square Garden*. The LP sold half a million copies in two months, and by year's end was certified triple-Platinum, with sales of over three million. It was Elvis' most successful album in nearly a decade. On the heels of the concert and album success, 'Burning Love'/'It's A Matter Of Time' was released August 1972, and quickly jumped to number two with sales over a million copies.

RCA shipped the single 'Separate Ways'/'Always On My Mind' in October. The song mirrored Elvis' personal life, with its tale of separation, and peaked at number 20 on the charts.

The April 1972 release of *He Touched Me* showcased Elvis' love for gospel music. Although it sold less than 200,000 copies, it earned Elvis a Grammy Award from the National Associate of Recording Arts and Sciences (NARAS) for Best Inspirational Performance at year's end.

January 12 and 14, 1973: Live Recordings for RCA; H.I.C. Arena, Honolulu, Hawaii

January 12

See See Rider (arranged by Elvis Presley)
Burning Love (Dennis Linde)
Something (George Harrison)
You Gave Me A Mountain (Marty Robbins)
Steamroller Blues (James Taylor)
My Way (Paul Anka/J. Reveaux/C. Francois)
Love Me (Jerry Leiber/Mike Stoller)
It's Over (Jimmie Rodgers)
Blue Suede Shoes (Carl Perkins)
I'm So Lonesome I Could Cry (Hank Williams)
Hound Dog (Jerry Leiber/Mike Stoller)
What Now My Love (C. Sigman/G. Becaud)
Fever (Davenport/Cooley)
Welcome To My World (R. Winkler/J. Hathcock)
Suspicious Minds (Mark James)

I'll Remember You (K. Lee)
An American Trilogy (Mickey Newberry)
A Big Hunk O'Love (Schroeder/Wyche)
Can't Help Falling In Love (Peretti/Creatore/Weiss)

January 14

See See Rider (Arranged by Elvis Presley)
Burning Love (Dennis Linde)
Something (George Harrison)
You Gave Me A Mountain (Marty Robbins)
Steamroller Blues (James Taylor)
My Way (Paul Anka/J. Reveaux/C. Francois)
Love Me (Jerry Leiber/Mike Stoller)
Johnny B. Goode (Chuck Berry)
It's Over (Jimmie Rodgers)
Blue Suede Shoes (Carl Perkins)
I'm So Lonesome I Could Cry (Hank Williams)
I Can't Stop Loving You (Don Gibson)
Hound Dog (Jerry Leiber/Mike Stoller)
What Now My Love (C. Sigman/G. Becaud)
Fever (Davenport/Cooley)
Welcome To My World (R. Winkler/J. Hathcock)
Suspicious Minds (Mark James)
I'll Remember You (K. Lee)
Long Tall Sally/Whole Lotta Shakin' Goin' On
    (E. Johnson – S. David)
An American Trilogy (Mickey Newberry)
A Big Hunk O'Love (Schroeder/Wyche)
Can't Help Falling In Love (Peretti/Creatore/Weiss)
Blue Hawaii (Leo Robin/Ralph Rainger)
Ku-U-I-Po (Peretti/Creatore/Weiss)
No More (Don Robertson/Hal Blair)
Hawaiian Wedding Song (King/Hoffman/Manning)
Early Morning Rain (Gordon Lightfoot)

Taped in Hawaii earlier in the year, the concert soundtrack album *Aloha From Hawaii Via Satellite* was released throughout the world in February 1972, two months before the special aired. The double album rose to number one on the LP charts and sold half a million copies in the first four weeks.

July 21–25, 1973: Studio Sessions for RCA, Stax Studios; Memphis, Tennessee

July 21

If You Don't Come Back (Jerry Leiber/Mike Stoller)
It's Diff'rent Now (Clive Westlake)
Three Corn Patches (Jerry Leiber/Mike Stoller)
Take Good Care Of Her (Ed Warren/Arthur Kent)

July 22

Find Out What's Happening (Jerry Crutchfield)
I've Got A Thing About You Baby (Tony Joe White)
Just A Little Bit (Thornton/Brown/Bass/Washington)

July 23

Raised On Rock (Mark James)
For Ol' Times Sake (Tony Joe White)

July 24

Girl Of Mine (Les Reed/Barry Mann)

July 25

Sweet Angeline (Arnold/Martin/Morrow)

September 22–23, 1973: Sessions for RCA, Elvis' Home; Palm Springs, California

I Miss You (Donnie Sumner)
Are You Sincere (Wayne Walker)

November 1973: Private Recordings, The Thompson House; Memphis, Tennessee

See See Rider (Arranged by Elvis Presley)
That's All Right (Arthur Crudup)
Baby What You Want Me To Do (Jimmy Reed)
Spanish Eyes (Kaempfert/Singleton/Snyder)
I'm So Lonesome I Could Cry (Hank Williams)

December 10–16, 1973: Studio Sessions for RCA, Stax Studio; Memphis, Tennessee

December 10

I Got A Feeling In My Body (Dennis Linde)
It's Midnight (Billy Edd Wheeler/Jerry Chesnut)

December 11

You Asked Me To (Waylon Jennings/Billy Joe Shaver)
If You Talk In Your Sleep (Red West/
    Johnny Christopher)

December 12

Mr. Songman (Donnie Sumner)
Thinking About You (Tim Baty)
Love Song Of The Year (Chris Christian)
Help Me (Larry Gatlin)

December 13

My Boy (B. Martin/P. Coulter)
Loving Arms (Tom Jans)
Good Time Charlie's Got The Blues (Danny O'Keefe)

December 14

Talk About The Good Times (Jerry Reed)

December 15

Promised Land (Chuck Berry)

Your Love's Been A Long Time Coming
    (Rory Bourke)
There's A Honky Tonk Angel (Troy Seals/Danny Rice)

December 16

If That Isn't Love (Dottie Rambo)
Spanish Eyes (B. Kaempfert/C. Singleton/E. Snyder)
She Wears My Ring (Boudleaux/Felice Bryant)

RCA provided Elvis with a mobile recording unit for his recordings at Stax Studios in Memphis in hopes of obtaining new material. The sessions yielded a couple of albums and singles, including 'Promised Land'/'It's Midnight', which rose to number 14, becoming Elvis' highest charting singles since 'Burning Love' – and the LP *Promised Land*.

March 20, 1974: Live Recordings for RCA, Mid–South Coliseum; Memphis, Tennessee

See See Rider (Traditional/arranged by Elvis Presley)
I Got A Woman/Amen (Ray Charles – J. Hairston)
Love Me (Jerry Leiber/Mike Stoller)
Trying To Get To You (Rose Marie McCoy/
    Charles Singleton)
All Shook Up (Otis Blackwell/Elvis Presley)
Steamroller Blues (James Taylor)
Teddy Bear/Don't Be Cruel (Kal Mann – Bernie Lowe)
Love Me Tender (Vera Matson/Elvis Presley)
Long Tall Sally/Whole Lotta Shakin' Goin' On/Mama
    Don't Dance/Flip, Flop and Fly/Jailhouse Rock/
    Hound Dog (Johnson/Penniman – Dave Williams/
    Sunny David – Ken Loggins/Jim Messina – Joe
    Turner – Jerry Leiber/Mike Stoller – Jerry Lieber/
    Mike Stoller)
Fever (Davenport/Cooley)

Polk Salad Annie (Tony Joe White)
Why Me Lord (Kris Kristofferson)
How Great Thou Art (Stuart K. Hine)
Suspicious Minds (Mark James)
Blueberry Hill/I Can't Stop Loving You
    (Lewis/Stock/Rose – Don Gibson)
Help Me (Larry Gatlin)
An American Trilogy (Mickey Newberry)
Let Me Be There (John Rostill)
My Baby Left Me (Arthur Crudup)
Lawdy, Miss Clawdy (Lloyd Price)
Funny How Time Slips Away (Willie Nelson)
Can't Help Falling In Love (Peretti/Creatore/Weiss)

August 16, 1974: Studio Rehearsals, RCA Studios; Hollywood, California

Softly As I Leave You (A. de Vita/H. Shaper)
The Twelfth Of Never (Jerry Livingston/Paul Francis
    Webster)

In November, National Academy of Recording Arts and Sciences (NARAS) awarded Elvis a Grammy for Best Inspirational Performance for "How Great Thou Art" from his LP *Elvis Recorded Live*.

Released in January, 'My Boy'/'Thinkin' About You' became Elvis' third Top 20 hit in a row.

March 10–12, 1975: Studio Sessions for RCA, RCA's Studio C; Hollywood, California

March 10

Fairytale (Anita Pointer/Bonnie Pointer)
Green, Green Grass Of Home (Claude Putnam, Jr)

I Can Help (Billy Swan)
And I Love You So (Don McLean)

March 11

Susan When She Tried (Don Reid)
T-R-O-U-B-L-E (Jerry Chesnut)
Tiger Man (J. H. Lous/S. Burns)
Woman Without Love (Jerry Chesnut)
Shake A Hand (Joe Morris)

March 12

Bringin' It Back (G. Gordon)
Pieces Of My Life (Troy Seals)

May 6, 1975: Live Recordings, Athletic Center; Murfreesboro, Tennessee

See See Rider (Traditional/arranged by Elvis Presley)
I Got A Woman/Amen (Ray Charles)

'T-R-O-U-B-L-E', from the to-be-released LP *Today*, and flip side 'Mr. Songman', from earlier recordings, were released in April and topped out at number 35. A month later, *Today* was released and utilised all new songs that Elvis recorded in March 1975.

June 5, 1975: Live Recordings, Hofheinz Pavilion; Houston, Texas

T-R-O-U-B-L-E (Jerry Chesnut)

June 6, 1975: Live Recordings, Memorial Auditorium; Dallas, Texas

Love Me (Jerry Leiber/Mike Stoller)
If You Love Me (Let Me Know) (John Rostill)
Love Me Tender (Vera Matson/Elvis Presley)

All Shook Up (Otis Blackwell/Elvis Presley)
(Let Me Be Your) Teddy Bear/Don't Be Cruel
    (K. Mann/B. Lowe − Otis Blackwell/Elvis Presley)
Hound Dog (Jerry Lieber/Mike Stoller)
The Wonder Of You (Baker Knight)
Burning Love (Dennis Linde)
Dialogue/Introductions/Johnny B. Goode
    (Chuck Berry)
How Great Thou Art (Stuart K. Hine)
Let Me Be There (John Rostill)
An American Trilogy (Mickey Newberry)

June 7, 1975: Live Recordings, Hirsch Memorial Coliseum; Shreveport, Louisiana

Funny How Time Slips Away (Willie Nelson)
Little Darlin' (Maurice Williams)
Mystery Train/Tiger Man (S. Phillips/Jr Parker −
    Joe Hill Louis/Sam Burns)
Can't Help Falling In Love (Peretti/Creatore Weiss)

June 9, 1975: Live Recordings, Mississippi Coliseum; Jackson, Mississippi

Why Me Lord (Kris Kristofferson)

Shipped at the end of September, 'Bringing It Back' with flip side 'Pieces of My Life' were pulled from the 10-track LP *Today* and sold only 60,000 copies.

December 13, 1975: Live Recordings; The Hilton, Las Vegas, Nevada

Softly As I Leave You (A. de Vita/H. Shaper)
America The Beautiful (arranged by Elvis Presley)

February 2–7, 1976: Sessions for RCA, The Jungle Room, Graceland; Memphis, Tennessee

February 2

Bitter They Are, Harder They Are (Larry Gatlin)
She Thinks I Still Care (Dickey Lee)
The Last Farewell (Roger Whittaker/R. A. Webster)

February 3

Solitaire (Neil Sedaka/Phil Cody)

February 4

Moody Blue (Mark James)
I'll Never Fall In Love Again (Lonnie Donegan/
    Jimmy Currie)

February 5

For The Heart (Dennis Linde)
Hurt (J/ Crane/A. Jacobs)
Danny Boy (Frederic Weatherly)

February 6

Never Again (Billy Edd Wheeler/Jerry Chesnut)
Love Coming Down (Jerry Chesnut)

February 7

Blue Eyes Crying In The Rain (Fred Rose)

Designed for the Elvis collector, *Elvis: A Legendary Performer,*
Vol. 2 combined rare recordings with legendary masters and a
souvenir booklet. Released in January 1977, the package sold
750,000 copies. In March, 'Hurt'/'For The Heart', from the
recent Graceland recording sessions, were released and sold a
quarter of a million copies. The uninspiring *From Elvis Presley
Boulevard, Memphis Tennessee* was released in April. The LP was
made up of songs from the Graceland recording sessions.

October 29–30, 1976: Sessions for RCA, The Jungle Room, Graceland; Memphis, Tennessee

October 29

It's Easy For You (Andrew Lloyd Webber/
    Tim Rice)
Way Down (Layng Martine, Jr)
Pledging My Love (F. Washington/D. Robey)

October 30

He'll Have To Go (Joe Allison/Audrey Allison)

With no new material ready for release, RCA pulled the last unreleased master, 'Moody Blue'/'She Thinks I Still Care', from the archives and shipped it out at the end of November. The record peaked at number 31 on the Top 100 chart, but was a number one country hit and sold more than 50,000 copies.

Increasingly behind in the delivery of new material to RCA, producer Felton Jarvis recorded Elvis' concerts in 1976 and early 1977. In another effort to try and get some new recordings, a make-shift studio was again set up at Graceland for recording. But at home, Elvis could not seem to focus on the task and often left the sessions to go to his bedroom. In March 1977, RCA put out a compilation of previously released material titled *My World*. Elvis' death, later in the year, propelled the album to Platinum status of over one millions copies sold.

March–May, 1977: Live Recordings for RCA, Various Concert Halls

Love Me Tender (Elvis Presley/Vera Matson)
Blue Suede Shoes (Carl Perkins)
That's All Right (Arthur Crudup)

Are You Lonesome Tonight? (Turk/Handman)
Blue Christmas (Bill Hayes/Jay Johnson)
Trying To Get To You (Rose Marie McCoy/
    Charles Singleton)
Lawdy, Miss Clawdy (Lloyd Price)
Jailhouse Rock (Jerry Leiber/Mike Stoller)
I Got A Woman/Amen (Ray Charles)
Fever (John Davenport/Eddie Cooley)
O Sole Mio/It's Now Or Never (Aaron
    Schroeder/Wally Gold)
Little Sister (Doc Pomus/Mort Shuman)
(Let Me Be Your) Teddy Bear/Don't Be Cruel
    (K. Mann/B. Lowe – Otis Blackwell/Elvis Presley)
Help Me (Larry Gatlin)

March 24 – Ann Arbor, Michigan

Unchained Melody (North/Zarat)
Little Darlin' (Maurice Williams)

March 24 – Saginaw, Michigan

If You Love Me (Let Me Know) (John Rostill)
Heartbreak Hotel (Mae Boren Axton/Tommy Durden/
    Elvis Presley)
Polk Salad Annie (Tony Joe White)
Hawaiian Wedding Song (King/Hoffman/Manning)
Bridge Over Troubled Water (Paul Simon)
Big Boss Man (Smith/Dixon)
Hound Dog (Jerry Leiber/Mike Stoller)

April 2 – Chicago, Illinois

My Way (Anka/Revaux/Francois)
Fairytale (Anita Pointer/Bonnie Pointer)
Mystery Train/Tiger Man (H. Parker, Jr – J. H. Louis/
    S. Burns)

June 19, 1977: Live Recordings for CBS's *Elvis In Concert*, Civic Auditorium; Omaha, Nebraska

See See Rider (Traditional/arranged by Elvis Presley)
I Got A Woman/Amen (Ray Charles)
That's All Right (Crudup)
Are You Lonesome Tonight? (Turk/Handman)
Love Me (Jerry Leiber/Mike Stoller)
Fairytale (Anita Pointer/Bonnie Pointer)
Little Sister (Doc Pomus/Mort Shuman)
(Let Me Be Your) Teddy Bear/Don't Be Cruel
      (K. Mann/B. Lowe – Otis Blackwell/Elvis Presley)
And I Love You So (Don McLean)
Jailhouse Rock (Jerry Leiber/Mike Stoller)
How Great Thou Art (Stuart K. Hine)
Early Morning Rain (Gordon Lightfoot)
What'd I Say (Ray Charles)
Johnny B. Goode (Chuck Berry)
I Really Don't Want To Know (Howard Barnes/
      Don Robertson)
Hurt (Crane/Jacobs)
Hound Dog (Jerry Leiber/Mike Stoller)
O Sole Mio/It's Now Or Never (Aaron
      Schroeder/Wally Gold)
Can't Help Falling In Love (Peretti/Creatore/Weiss)

June 21, 1977: Live Recordings for CBS's *Elvis In Concert*, Rushmore Civic Center; Rapid City, South Dakota

See See Rider (Traditional/Arranged by Elvis Presley)
I Got A Woman/Amen (Ray Charles)
That's All Right (Crudup)
Are You Lonesome Tonight? (Turk/Handman)
Love Me (Jerry Leiber/Mike Stoller)

If You Love Me (Let Me Know) (John Rostill)
You Gave Me A Mountain (Marty Robbins)
Jailhouse Rock (Jerry Leiber/Mike Stoller)
O Sole Mio/It's Now Or Never (Aaron Schroeder/
    Wally Gold)
Trying To Get To You (Rose Marie McCoy/
    Charles Singleton)
Hawaiian Wedding Song (King/Hoffman/Manning)
(Let Me Be Your) Teddy Bear/Don't Be Cruel
    (K. Mann/B. Lowe – Otis Blackwell/Elvis Presley)
My Way (Anka/Revaux/Francois)
Early Morning Rain (Gordon Lightfoot)
What'd I Say (Ray Charles)
Johnny B. Goode (Chuck Berry)
I Really Don't Want To Know (Howard Barnes/
    Don Robertson)
Hurt (Crane/Jacobs)
Hound Dog (Jerry Leiber/Mike Stoller)
Unchained Melody (North/Zaret)
Can't Help Falling In Love (Peretti/Creatore/Weiss)

In July 1977, 'Way Down'/'Pledging My Love' was released and rose to number one on *Billboard*'s country chart, number 18 on the Top 100, and became Elvis' seventeenth number one on the UK charts. It was the last single released before Elvis' death and sold almost a millions copies. The LP *Moody Blue* – made up of songs recorded at Graceland, during Elvis' spring tour, and the previously released 'Let Me Be There' – was also released in July. Following Elvis' death, the album became his most successful in almost five years, selling more than two million copies.

Six days after Elvis' death, on August 16, 1977, RCA reported they had sold over eight million of his recordings since his death. 'Way Down' was certified Gold by RIAA in September

1977. In answer to public demand, *Elvis In Concert* was released in October 1977 and was quickly certified Platinum, selling 1.5 million copies.

In 1979, it was discovered that Elvis was not a member of Broadcast Music Inc., one of three companies that collect artist performance money, and thus had probably lost millions of dollars in royalty payments.

Elvis was posthumously inducted into the Rock and Roll Hall of Fame in Cleveland in 1986.

Four of Elvis' songs were inducted into the NARAS Hall of Fame: (1) the 1956 recording of 'Hound Dog' in 1988; (2) the 1956 recording of 'Heartbreak Hotel' in 1995; (3) the 1954 recording of 'That's All Right Mama' in 1998; and (4) the 1969 recording of 'Suspicious Minds' in 1999.

In 1998, Elvis was posthumously inducted into the Country Music Hall of Fame.

Elvis On Film

Love Me Tender

1956

Twentieth-Century Fox
Working Title: The Reno Brothers

Plot:

Clint Reno, the youngest of four brothers, works the family farm while his elder siblings go off to fight for the Confederate Army during the American Civil War. At war's end, he marries the girlfriend of his eldest brother, who is presumed dead. Trouble arises when the brother returns home. Clint dies in a dispute over the return of stolen Federal money.

Songs:

'Let Me'
'Love Me Tender' . . . the single reached number one
in the charts before the film even opened.
'Poor Boy'
'We're Gonna Move'

Trivia:

1. The title song 'Love Me Tender' provided new lyrics to the Civil War-era ballad 'Aura Lee'. The single sold over 1,000,000 copies in advance orders.
2. The role of Clint Reno was expanded specifically for Elvis' film debut from 4 or 5 lines in the original script.
3. Elvis memorised the entire script prior to arriving in Hollywood.

4. Originally excited that his film debut was to be a strictly dramatic role, Elvis was disappointed when the studio later decided to add some songs.

Loving You

1957

> Paramount Pictures
> Working Titles: Running Wild; Something for the
> Girls; The Lonesome Cowboy

Plot:

Singing gas station attendant Deke Rivers is discovered by a female music promoter, who changes his name to Jimmy Thompson and grooms him for fame and fortune as a teen idol. When the press labels him a bad influence, he must convince them of his sincerity.

Songs:

> 'Got A Lot Of Livin' To Do'
> 'Hot Dog'
> '(Let Me Be Your) Teddy Bear' . . . the single rose to
> number one in the charts.
> '(Let's Have A) Party'
> 'Lonesome Cowboy'
> 'Loving You' . . . as the B-side to 'Teddy Bear', it
> charted at number 28 on its own.
> 'Mean Woman Blues' . . . did not chart, but received
> extensive radio airplay.

Trivia:

The film role was essentially a fictionalised account of Elvis' own career.

Vernon and Gladys Presley were cast as audience members in the climactic concert scene.

Elvis could not watch the film again after his mother died.

Although the single only reached number 28, both the EP and LP charted at number one.

Jail House Rock

1957

MGM

Plot:

Vince Edwards, an angry ex-con who learned to play guitar while in prison, becomes a singer upon his release. Disillusioned with the music business, he forms his own record label and becomes an overnight sensation. When success goes to his head, Vince almost forgets the people who helped him achieve it.

Songs:

'Don't Leave Me Now'

'I Want To Be Free'

'Jailhouse Rock' . . . both the single and the EP
      rocketed to number one in the charts.

'Treat Me Nice' . . . as the flip side to 'Jailhouse
      Rock', it reached number 27 in the charts.

'Young And Beautiful'

'(You're So Square) Baby I Don't Care'

Trivia:

1. 'Jailhouse Rock' was the first song to enter the UK singles charts at number one.
2. Actor/dancer Gene Kelly applauded Elvis' performance following the filming of the famous Jailhouse Rock dance sequence.
3. Leading lady Judy Tyler was killed in an automobile accident before the film was released.
4. *Jailhouse Rock* ranked number 14 in ticket sales for the year.

King Creole

1958

Paramount Pictures
Working Titles: A Stone for Danny Fisher; Sing, You
Sinners

Plot:

Against his father's wishes, Danny Fisher drops out of college to become a nightclub singer on New Orleans' famed Bourbon Street. All goes well until he gets involved with a mobster's girlfriend.

Songs:

'As Long As I Have You'
'Crawfish'
'Dixieland Rock'
'Don't Ask Me Why' . . . as the B-side to 'Hard
Headed Woman', it reached number 28.
'Hard Headed Woman' . . . rose to number two on the
singles charts.
'King Creole'
'Lover Doll'
'New Orleans'
'Steadfast, Loyal And True'
'Trouble'
'Young Dreams
'Danny' . . . dropped when film title changed; not
released until 1978.

Trivia:

1. Elvis' role was originally conceived for James Dean.
2. Leading lady Dolores Hart joined a convent soon after making this film.

3. Director Michael Curtiz also directed *Casablanca* and *Mildred Pierce*.
4. Colonel Parker got Elvis a draft deferment in order to complete filming.
5. Both *King Creole* EPs chart at number one, while the LP reaches number two.

G.I. Blues

1960

> Paramount Pictures
> Working Title: Café' Europa

Plot:

Tulsa McClean, a U.S. Army soldier stationed in Germany, wants to open a nightclub when he gets out of the service. He makes a bet he can bed a cabaret dancer with a reputation for being hard to get, but tries to back out of the bet when he finds himself falling for her, even though it means losing the money to fund his dream.

Songs:

> 'Big Boots'
> 'Blue Suede Shoes'
> 'Didja Ever'
> 'Doin' The Best I Can'
> 'Frankfort Special'
> 'G.I. Blues'
> 'Pocketful Of Rainbows'
> 'Shoppin' Around'
> 'Tonight's All Right For Love'
> 'What's She Really Like'
> 'Wooden Heart' . . . used as the B-side to a single five
> >years later.

Trivia:

1. This was Elvis' first film after returning from military service.
2. *G.I. Blues* ranked number 14 in box office receipts for the year.
3. Although the film produced no singles, the LP rose to number one in the charts.

Flaming Star

1960

> 20th Century Fox
> Working Titles: Black Star; Black Heart; Flaming Star; Flaming Lance

Plot:

Able to find peace in neither the world of his Native American mother nor his white father, Pacer Burton sides with the Kiowa Indians in a land dispute against his white half-brother.

Songs:

> 'A Cane And A High Starched Collar'
> 'Flaming Star'
> 'Black Star' . . . recorded as 'Flaming Star' when film title was changed; released in 1991.
> 'Britches' . . . cut from film; released in 1978.
> 'Summer Kisses, Winter Tears' . . . cut from film when it drew laughter during previews.

Trivia:

1. Marlon Brando and Frank Sinatra were originally considered for the lead role.
2. Leading lady Barbara Eden later achieved fame in TV's *I Dream Of Jeannie*.
3. The EP *Elvis By Request – Flaming Star* charted at number 14.

Wild In The Country

1961

20th Century Fox
Working Title: Lonely Man

Plot:

Troubled bad boy Glen Tyler discovers he has talent when a psychologist encourages him in a literary career. In between, he juggles the attentions of three very different types of women: the wholesome girl next door, the bad girl with a past, and the older woman.

Songs:

'I Slipped, I Stumbled, I Fell'
'In My Way'
'Wild In The Country' . . . reached number 26 in the
      singles charts.
'Forget Me Never' . . . cut from film.
'Lonely Man' . . . cut from film.

Trivia:

1. A new ending had to be filmed when preview audiences found the suicide of the older girlfriend too harsh.
2. Songs were hastily inserted into the storyline to avoid the poor ticket sales that plagued *Flaming Star*.

Blue Hawaii

1961

Paramount Pictures
Working Title: Beach Boy

Plot:

Chad Gates returns from the army to his former life of surf

boards and beach buddies. When his parents pressure him to run the family's pineapple plantation, he goes to work as a guide at his girlfriend's tourist agency.

Songs:

'Almost Always True'
'Aloha Oe'
'Beach Boy Blues'
'Blue Hawaii'
'Can't Help Falling In Love' . . . peaked at number
    two in the singles charts.
'Hawaiian Sunset'
'Hawaiian Wedding Song'
'Island Of Love'
'Ito Eats'
'Ku–U–I–Po'
'Moonlight Swim'
'No More'
'Rock-a-Hula Baby' . . . as the flip side to 'Can't Help
    Falling In Love', it charted at number 23.
'Slicin' Sand'
'Steppin' Out Of Line'

Trivia:

1. Angela Landsbury, who plays the mother, was only 10 years older than Elvis.
2. The album spent 20 weeks at number one in the charts, a record unbroken until 1977.
3. *Blue Hawaii* was ranked number 14 in box office receipts for the year.

Follow That Dream

1962

United Artists

Working Titles: Pioneer, Go Home; Here Come The
   Kwimpers; It's A Beautiful Life; What A
   Wonderful Life

Plot:

Tony Kwimper and his father run out of gas along a Florida
highway and decide to set up roadside housekeeping. All goes
well until a meddlesome social worker tries to take away the
Kwimper family of assorted cast-off children.

Songs:

'Angel'
'Follow That Dream'
'I'm Not The Marrying Kind'
'Sound Advice'
'What A Wonderful Life'

Trivia:

1. This performance got Elvis some of his best reviews.
2. Singer/songwriter Tom Petty says he decided to become a
   musician after seeing this film.
3. The EP *Follow That Dream* charted at number 15.

Kid Galahad

1962

United Artists

Plot:

Just out of military service, Walter Gulik arrives in town
looking for a job and finds two: mechanic and sparring partner.
His surprise knock-out punch sets him on a boxing career that is
marred by corruption.

Songs:

'A Whistling Tune'

'Home Is Where The Heart Is'
'I Got Lucky'
'King Of The Whole Wide World'
'Riding The Rainbow'
'This Is Living'

Trivia:

1. Tough-guy actor Charles Bronson was not happy about playing a role in an Elvis film.
2. Elvis was embarrassed by how fat he looked onscreen.
3. The *Kid Galahad* EP charted at number 30.
4. The film was ranked number 37 in box office receipts for the year.

Girls! Girls! Girls!

1962

Paramount Pictures
Working Titles: A Girl In Every Port; Gumbo Ya-Ya;
    Welcome Aboard

Plot:

Singing tuna fisherman Ross Carpenter tries to buy back the fishing boat that he and his father built. Dockside, he is tangled up with two women.

Songs:

'A Boy Like Me, A Girl Like You'
'Because Of Love'
'Earth Boy'
'Girls! Girls! Girls!'
'I Don't Wanna Be Tied'
'Return To Sender' . . . reached number two in the
    singles charts.
'Song Of The Shrimp'

'Thanks To The Rolling Sea'
'The Walls Have Ears'
'We'll Be Together'
'We're Comin' In Loaded'
'Dainty Little Moonbeams' . . . cut from film; released
in 1993.
'I Don't Want To' . . . cut from film.
'Where Do You Come From' . . . cut from film, but
used as B-side on 'Return to Sender'.

Trivia:

1. The soundtrack album reached number three on the LP charts with sales of 600,000 copies.
2. Despite Elvis' discontent with the roles and songs he was offered, his films were actually much better than the teen exploitation movies being made by other pop stars of the time.
3. *Girls! Girls! Girls!* was ranked number 31 in box office receipts for the year.

It Happened At The World's Fair

1963

MGM
Working Title: Mister, Will You Marry Me?

Plot:

Mike Edwards is co-owner of a crop-duster that his partner loses in a card game. The two hitch hike to the World's Fair, where the partner attempts to win the money to redeem the airplane in a poker game. Mike gets saddled with an Asian girl lost from her father, but finds time to romance a young nurse.

Songs:

'A World Of Our Own'

'Beyond The Bend'
'Cotton Candy Land'
'Happy Ending'
'How Would You Like To Be?'
'I'm Falling In Love Tonight'
'One Broken Heart For Sale' . . . reached number 11
    in the singles charts.
'Relax'
'Take Me To The Fair'
'They Remind Me Too Much Of You' . . . charted at
    number 53 as the single's B-side.

Trivia:

1. Film was shot on location at the World's Fair in Seattle, Washington.
2. The costume designer was shocked to discover that Elvis never wore underwear.
3. Kurt Russell made his screen debut as a bratty kid who kicks Elvis in the shin.
4. The soundtrack album *It Happened At The World's Fair* reached number four in the LP charts.
5. The film ranked number 55 in ticket sales for the year.

Fun In Acapulco

1963

Paramount Pictures
Working Title: Vacation In Acapulco

Plot:

Mike Windgren, a former trapeze artist battling a fear of heights after an accident, signs on as a deck hand aboard a boat headed for South America. When he gets stranded in Acapulco, he lands a job as a lifeguard/singer at a hotel, where a rivalry develops with another lifeguard (a champion cliff diver) over the hotel's social director. Mike wins the girl and overcomes his fear of heights by diving off a cliff.

Songs:

> 'Bossa Nova Baby' . . . rose to number eight in the singles charts.
> 'El Toro'
> 'Fun In Acapulco'
> 'Guadalahara'
> 'I Think I'm Gonna Like It Hear'
> 'Marguerita'
> 'Mexico'
> 'The Bullfighter Was A Lady'
> '(There's) No Room To Rhumba In A Sports Car'
> 'Vino, Dinero y Amor'
> 'You Can't Say No In Acapulco'

Trivia:

1. Despite extensive use of background footage, all of Elvis' scenes were shot in Hollywood.
2. The *Fun In Acapulco* soundtrack album peaked at number three in the LP charts.

Kissin' Cousins

1964

> MGM

Soldier Josh Morgan tries to convince his hillbilly look-alike cousin Jodie Tatum to allow the army to build a missile site on his land. The action is livened up by a pack of man-hunting mountain girls called the Kittyhawks.

Songs:

> 'Anyone (Could Fall In Love With You)'
> 'Barefoot Ballad'

'Catchin' On Fast'

'Echoes Of Love'

'(It's A) Long Lonely Highway'

'Kissin' Cousins' . . . rose to number 12 on the singles charts.

'Once Is Enough'

'One Boy, Two Little Girls'

'Tender Feeling'

'There's Gold In The Mountains'

'Smokey Mountain Boy'

Trivia:

1. Elvis played both Josh and Jodie, a twin theme his films returned to several times.
2. Elvis hated the dark-blond wig he wore as country cousin Jodie because it was so close to his own natural colour.
3. The *Kissin' Cousins* soundtrack reached number six in the album charts.
4. The film ended the year ranked at number 26 in movie ticket sales.

Viva Las Vegas

1964

MGM

Working Title: Only Girl in Town; Love in Las Vegas (used for UK release)

Plot:

Singing race car driver Lucky Jackson arrives in town for the Vegas Grand Prix, but needs money to replace his engine. He finds a job at a hotel, where he is distracted by co-worker Ann-Margret and becomes rivals with another racer.

Songs:

'C'mon, Everybody'
'If You Think I Don't Need You'
'I Need Somebody To Lean On'
'Santa Lucia'
'The Lady Loves Me'
'The Yellow Rose Of Texas/The Eyes Of Texas'
'Today, Tomorrow And Forever'
'Viva Las Vegas' . . . as the flip side of the single, it
    reached number 29 on its own.
'What'd I Say' . . . peaked at number 21 on the singles
    charts.
'Do The Vega' . . . cut from the film
'Night Life' . . . cut from the film
'You're The Boss' . . . cut from the film

Trivia:

1. This was Elvis' highest grossing film, ranked at number 11 in ticket sales for the year.
2. The onscreen chemistry between Elvis and Ann-Margret reflects their off screen romance.
3. 'If You Think I Don't Need You' was written by Memphis Mafia member Red West.
4. Colonel Parker had three numbers Elvis performed with Ann-Margret cut from the film because he feared she was stealing the show away from his client.
5. Photos from the wedding scene were included in a press article stating that Elvis and Ann-Margret had secretly married.
6. At number 92, the *Viva Las Vegas* soundtrack album barely got into the charts.

Roustabout

1964

Paramount Pictures

Plot:

Charlie Rogers is a drifter who wants to become a singer. When his motorcycle breaks down, he gets a job at a local carnival to earn money for repairs. His singing draws a crowd, saving the carnival from foreclosure. When Charlie's cycle is fixed, the carnival owner enlists the help of a pretty girl to convince him to stay.

Songs:

'Big Love, Big Heartache'
'Carny Town'
'Hard Knocks'
'It's A Wonderful World'
'It's Carnival Time'
'Little Egypt'
'One Track Heart'
'Poison Ivy League'
'Roustabout'
'There's A Brand New Day On The Horizon'
'Wheels On My Heels'
'I'm A Roustabout' . . . not used in film; rediscovered in 2003.

Trivia:

1. The role of the carnival owner, played by Barbara Stanwyck, was originally offered to Mae West.
2. When Elvis received a head wound while performing his own stunts, the injury was worked into the storyline.
3. Colonel Parker drew upon his years as a carny to provide authenticity to the script.

4. Despite the lack of quality songs, the soundtrack album rose to number one in the charts.
5. *Roustabout* was ranked number 28 in box office receipts for the year 1965.

Girl Happy

1965

MGM

Plot:

Singer Rusty Wells is hired to chaperone a gangster's teenage daughter on spring break in Florida. He must intervene when the girl falls for a womanising cad.

Songs:

'Cross My Heart And Hope To Die'
'Do Not Disturb'
'Do The Clam' . . . hit number 21 in the singles charts.
'Fort Lauderdale Chamber of Commerce'
'Girl Happy'
'I've Got To Find My Baby'
'Puppet On A String' . . . peaked at number 14 in the singles charts.
'Spring Fever'
'Startin' Tonight'
'The Meanest Girl In Town'
'Wolf Call'

Trivia:

1. Elvis' singing voice is higher than normal due to a recording speed error.
2. 'The Meanest Girl in Town' was originally recorded by Bill Hailey and the Comets as 'Yeah She's Evil'.

3. The soundtrack album peaked at number eight in the charts, despite poor sound quality.
4. *Girl Happy* ranked number 25 in ticket sales for the year.

Tickle Me

1965

Allied Artists Pictures Corporation

Plot:

Singing rodeo cowboy Lonnie Beale moonlights at a desert beauty spa and gets involved with a score of beautiful women, helping one to search for lost gold in a nearby ghost town.

Songs:

'Dirty, Dirty Feeling'
'I Feel That I've Known You Forever'
'I'm Yours' . . . reached number 11 in the singles charts.
'It Feels So Right' . . . charted at number 55 as the B-side to '(Such an) Easy Question'.
'(It's A) Long Lonely Highway' . . . used as the flip side to 'I'm Yours'.
'Night Rider'
'Put The Blame On Me'
'Slowly But Surely'
'(Such An) Easy Question' . . . rose to number 11 in the singles charts.

Trivia:

1. To save money, the film used songs that had been recorded between 1960 and 1963, but had never been released.
2. Ticket sales saved the foundering film company from bankruptcy.
3. Elvis' $750,000 salary accounted for half of the film's budget.

Harum Scarum

1965

MGM

Working Title: Harem Holiday (used for UK release)

Plot:

Singing matinee idol Johnny Tyronne is kidnapped by assassins while promoting his latest movie in a Middle Eastern kingdom. Believing that Johnny can kill with his bare hands, the assassins coerce him into killing the king in return for the lives of assorted orphans and slave girls to whom the actor has become attached, one of whom is the king's own daughter.

Songs:

'Animal Instinct'
'Go East Young Man'
'Golden Coins'
'Hey Little Girl'
'My Desert Serenade'
'Shake That Tambourine'
'So Close, Yet So Far (from Paradise)'
'Wisdom Of The Ages'
'Harem Holiday' . . . cut from film when title changed.
'Kismet' . . . cut from film.
'Mirage' . . . cut from film.

Trivia:

1. The filming schedule was so short that Elvis offered to fake illness in order to buy the director additional time.
2. After seeing a preview, Colonel Parker suggested the addition of a talking camel in order to make audiences think the film was supposed to be campy.
3. 'Shake That Tambourine' required 35 takes to get it right. Elvis hated the song.

4. Despite the poor quality of the songs, the soundtrack album charted at number eight.

5. *Harum Scarum* ranked number 40 for the year in ticket sales.

Frankie And Johnny

1966

United Artists

Plot:

Johnny, a riverboat entertainer and compulsive gambler, trades in his girlfriend Frankie for a new Lady Luck, with near-fatal results.

Songs:

'Beginner's Luck'

'Chesay'

'Come Along'

'Down By The Riverside/When The Saints Go Marching In'

'Everybody Come Aboard'

'Frankie And Johnny' . . . reached number 25 in the singles charts.

'Hard Luck'

'Look Out Broadway'

'Petunia, The Gardner's Daughter'

'Please Don't Stop Loving Me' . . . cut from film; used for B-side of single; charts at number 45.

'Shout It Out'

'What Every Woman Lives For'

Trivia:

1. Leading lady Donna Douglas tried to shed her Ellie Mae Clampett character from TV's *The Beverly Hillbillies*.

2. The film was envisioned as a spoof of silent film legend Rudolph Valentino's *The Sheik*.
3. *Frankie and Johnny* ranked number 48 in ticket sales, and number 20 on the album charts.

Paradise, Hawaiian Style

1966

Paramount Pictures

Plot:

Pilot Rick Richards is grounded, forcing his partner in their charter helicopter service to take over the flying duties. When the partner and his little girl crash, it's Rick to the rescue.

Songs:

'A Dog's Life'
'Datin''
'Drums Of The Islands'
'House Of Sand'
'Paradise, Hawaiian Style'
'Queenie Wahine's Papaya'
'Sand Castles'
'Scratch My Back (Then I'll Scratch Yours)'
'Stop Where You Are'
'This Is My Heaven'

Trivia:

1. After the drop in ticket sales from the last few films, the studio tried to return to the successful formula of *Blue Hawaii*.
2. Petula Clark was originally offered the female lead role.
3. *Paradise, Hawaiian Style* ranked number 40 in box office sales for the year.
4. Despite the lack of singles, the soundtrack album managed to chart at number 15.

Spinout

1966

MGM
Working Titles: Raceway; and about eight more.

Plot:

Mike McCoy is the lead singer in a pop group and a part-time race car driver. He his pursued by three women: his group's female drummer, a spoiled rich girl, and a best-selling author. Object: matrimony.

Songs:

'Adam And Evil'
'All That I Am' . . . charted at number 41 as the flip side to 'Spinout'.
'Am I Ready'
'Beach Shack'
'I'll Be Back'
'Never Say Yes'
'Smorgasbord'
'Spinout' . . . peaked at number 40 in the singles charts.
'Stop, Look And Listen'

Trivia:

1. Colonel Parker thought the original title *Never Say No* was too suggestive.
2. This is the last year Elvis was listed in the Top 10 of box office draws.
3. *Spinout* ranked a disappointing number 57 in ticket sales for the year.
4. The soundtrack album charted at number 18 with sales of 300,000 copies.

Easy Come, Easy Go

1967

Paramount Pictures

Plot:

Former Navy Seal frogman Ted Jackson dives for buried treasure with the help of a nightclub owner and a dancer.

Songs:

'Easy Come, Easy Go'
'I'll Take Love'
'Sing You Children'
'She's A Machine'
'The Love Machine'
'Yoga Is As Yoga Does'
'You Gotta Stop'

Trivia:

1. This is the only Elvis film to lose money.
2. Not coincidentally, this is the last film Elvis made with Paramount.
3. *Easy Come, Easy Go* was ranked number 50 in ticket sales for the year.
4. The soundtrack EP failed to even chart, and was the last EP Elvis made.

Double Trouble

1967

MGM

Working Title: You're Killing Me

Plot:

While in London on tour, rock singer Guy Lambert gets

involved with a femme fatale and a teenage heiress, whose jewel–smuggler uncle is after her money.

Songs:

> 'Baby If You'll Give Me All Of Your Love'
> 'City By Night'
> 'Could I Fall in Love'
> 'Double Trouble'
> 'I Love Only One Girl'
> 'It Won't Be Long'
> 'Long Legged Girl (With the Short Dress On)' . . .
>> peaked at number 63 in the singles charts.
> 'Old MacDonald'
> 'There's So Much World To See'

Trivia:

1. Elvis plays his own double in the film; another example of the twin theme.
2. Ticket sales ranking falls to number 58 for the year.
3. The *Double Trouble* soundtrack album barely reached number 47 in the charts.

Clambake

1967

> MGM
> Working Title: Too Big For Texas

Plot:

Scott Heyward, the heir to a Texas oil fortune, switches places with Tom Wilson, a Florida water ski instructor, to see whether girls will like him for himself, rather than his father's money.

Songs:

> 'A House That Has Everything'
> 'Clambake'

'Confidence'

'Hey, Hey, Hey'

'Who Needs Money'

'How Can You Lose What You Never Had' . . . cut
from film

'The Girl I Never Loved' . . . cut from film

Trivia

1. The title was originally suggested by Colonel Parker for *Spinout*.
2. Filming was delayed for 11 days when Elvis suffered a concussion in a fall at home.
3. The *Clambake* album charted at a disappointing number 40.

Stay Away, Joe

1968

MGM

Plot:

Womanising Navajo rodeo rider Joe Lightcloud narrowly avoids irate boyfriends and a shotgun wedding while persuading a Congressman to give his family some cattle.

Songs:

'All I Needed Was The Rain'

'Dominick'

'Stay Away, Joe' . . . charted at number 67 as the
B-side to 'U.S. Male'.

Trivia:

1. Elvis so hated the song 'Dominick', which he sang to a bull onscreen, that he begged that it never be released on a record. It was, however, in 1994.
2. The film finished at number 68 in ticket sales for the year.

Speedway

1968

MGM

Plot:

Playboy stock car racer Steve Grayson must raise $145,000 fast when the IRS questions why his bumbling manager has failed to file a tax return. Between races he romances the IRS agent sent to investigate him.

Songs:

'Goin' Home'
'He's Your Uncle, Not Your Dad'
'Let Yourself Go' . . . released as the flip side to 'Your Time Hasn't Come Yet, Baby'.
'Mine'
'Speedway'
'There Ain't Nothing Like A Song'
'Who Are You, Who Am I'
'Your Time Hasn't Come Yet, Baby' . . . barely hit number 71 in the singles charts.
'Five Sleepy Heads' . . . cut from film
'Suppose' . . . cut from film
'Western Union' . . . cut from film

Trivia:

1. Nancy 'These Boots Are Made For Walking' Sinatra plays the female lead.
2. The film was originally offered to Sonny and Cher.
3. Racecar driver Richard Petty has a cameo role.
4. The *Speedway* album, charting at number 82, was lowest ranking yet.
5. The film ranked number 40 in box office receipts for the year.

Live A Little, Love A Little

1968

MGM

Plot:

Stranded newspaper photographer Greg Nolan is nursed back to health by the pretty screwball owner of a beach house. Strapped for cash, he tries to juggle two jobs, one with a posh ad agency and another with the girly magazine *Classic Cat*, but has trouble finding time to do both.

Songs:

'A Little Less Conversation' . . . hit number 69 in the singles charts.

'Almost In Love' . . . charted at number 95 as the flip side to the single.

'Edge Of Reality' . . . released as the B-side to 'If I Can Dream', which reached number 12.

'Wonderful World'

Trivia:

1. Vernon Presley has a cameo role as a photo shoot model.
2. Elvis' own Great Dane, Brutus, played the role of Albert in the film.

Charro!

1969

National General Pictures

Working Title: Come Sundown, Come Hell

Plot:

Ex-gunslinger Jess Wade, falsely accused of murder and the theft of a valuable cannon from Mexican revolutionaries, tries to prove his innocence by tracking down his former gang who committed the crimes.

Songs:

> 'Charro!' . . . the title song was added at the last
>> minute; released as B-side to 'Memories'.

Trivia:

This gritty western was the closest Elvis came to the dramatic role he always wanted.

The Trouble With Girls

1969

> MGM
> Working Titles: The Chautauqua; The Trouble With
>> Girls (And How To Get Into It)

Plot:

Walter Hale, the owner of a travelling medicine show, mingles with eccentric small town folks in 1920s Iowa, while trying to solve the murder of a local womaniser.

Songs:

> 'Almost'
> 'Clean Up Your Own Backyard' . . . peaked at number
>> 35 on the singles charts.
> 'Signs Of The Zodiac'
> 'Swing Down Sweet Chariot'
> 'The Whiffenpoof Song'
> 'Violet (Flower of NYU)'

Change Of Habit

1969

> Universal

Plot:

John Carpenter, an idealistic young doctor working in the

ghetto, unknowingly romances a young postulant who has been secretly sent to work at his clinic prior to taking her vows. Will she choose God or Elvis?

Songs:

> 'Change Of Habit'
> 'Have A Happy'
> 'Just For Old Time Sake' . . . recorded in 1962.
> 'Let's Be Friends' . . . cut from film.
> 'Let Us Pray'
> 'Mine' . . . recorded in 1967; cut from *Speedway*.
> 'Rubberneckin'' . . . recorded in Memphis in 1969;
> > used as B-side to 'Don't Cry Daddy'.

Trivia:

1. To save money, the studio originally planned to recycle songs that had been previously recorded. In the end, four new songs were added, although one of those was later cut.
2. Mary Tyler Moore appeared as the young nun, while in a career slump between the hit TV shows *The Dick Van Dyke Show* (1961–66) and *The Mary Tyler Moore Show* (1970–77).
3. Elvis frequently used this character's name as an alias when checking into hotels and booking airline flights.

Main References Sources

Braun, Eric. *Elvis Presley Film Encyclopedia*. Overlook Press, 1997.

Brown, Peter H. and Pat H. Boeske. *Down At The End Of Lonely Street*. E. P. Dutton, 1997.

Clayton, Marie. *Elvis Presley, Unseen Archives*. Barnes & Noble Books, 2004.

Curtin, Jim with Renata Ginter. *Elvis, Unknown Stories Behind The Legend*. Celebrity Books, 1998.

Davis, Arthur. *Elvis Presley, Quote Unquote*. Crescent Books, 1995.

Dundy, Elaine. *Elvis And Gladys*. McMillian Publishing Co., 1985.

Elvis By The Presleys. Documentary. 2005

Elvis – The '68 Comeback Special. Bmg Distribution, 2004.

Elvis. CBS miniseries, 2005.

Freedman, Favius. *Meet Elvis Presley*. Scholastic Book Service, 1971.

Goldmine Magazine. Kraus Publications.

Guralnick, Peter and Ernst Jorgensen. *Elvis Day By Day: The Definitive Record Of His Life And Music*. Ballantine Books, 1999.

Guralnick, Peter. *Careless Love: The Unmaking Of Elvis Presley*. Little Brown & Co., 1999.

Guralnick, Peter. *Last Train to Memphis: The Rise Of Elvis Presley*. Little Brown & Co., 1994.

Hammertree, Patsy Guy. *Elvis Presley: A Biography*. Greenwood Press, 1985.

Jorgensen, Ernst. *Elvis Presley, A Life In Music, The Complete Recording Sessions*. St Martin's Press, 1998.

McKeon, Elizabeth and Linda Everett. *Elvis Speaks*. Cumberland House Publishing, Inc., 1997.

Modern Screen Presents Elvis – His Life Story. Sterling Magazine, 1979.

Presley, Priscilla. *Elvis And Me*. Berkley Publishing Group, revised edition, 1991.

Presleys, The, edited by David Ritz. *Elvis By The Presleys*. Crown Publishers, 2005.

Rovin, Jeff. *The World According To Elvis, Quotes From The King*. Harper Paperbacks, 1992.

The Elvis Interviews 1955–1977, Recorded Interviews With The King Of Rock 'N Roll. Radio Spirits, Inc., 2004.

Simpson, Paul. *The Rough Guide To Elvis*. Penguin Books, Ltd, 2002.

Slaughter, Todd with Anne E. Nixon. *The Elvis Archives*. Omnibus Press, 2004.

Various magazines, newspapers and websites.

Various televised interviews with Priscilla Presley and Lisa Marie Presley.